KNIGHTS
IRON OF THE CROSS

KNIGHTS OF THE IRON CROSS

A History 1939-1945

GORDON WILLIAMSON

BLANDFORD PRESS

LONDON · NEW YORK · SYDNEY

First published in the UK by Blandford Press,
Artillery House, Artillery Row, London SW1P 1RT

Reprinted 1987

Copyright © 1987 Gordon Williamson

Distributed in the United States by
Sterling Publishing Co., Inc.,
2 Park Avenue, New York, N.Y. 10016

Distributed in Australia by
Capricorn Link (Australia) Pty Ltd,
P O Box 665, Lane Cove, NSW 2066

ISBN 0-7137-1820-X

Editor : M.G. Burns

Typeset by Best-set Typesetter Limited
Printed in Great Britain by
Biddles Ltd., Guildford and Kings Lynn

CONTENTS

NOTE

Readers may wish to note that photographs and/or text on the following *Ritterkreuzträger* are featured in *The Iron Cross — A History 1813–1957* by the same author, also published by Blandford Press.

Oberfeldwebel Martin Beilig
Korvettenkapitän Heinrich Bleichrodt
SS-Obersturmbannführer Gerd Bremer
Grossadmiral Karl Dönitz
Leutnant Otto Engel
Generalleutnant Adolf Galland
Oberst Hans Jordan
Oberwachtmeister Wilhelm Kessel
SS-Hauptsturmführer Fritz Klingenberg
Korvettenkapitän Otto Kretschmer
Oberleutnant Ekkehard Kylling-Schmidt
Kapitän zur See Wolfgang Lüth
SS-Hauptsturmführer Heinz Macher
General Eugen Meindl
SS-Obersturmbannführer Kurt Meyer
SS-Standartenführer Johannes Mühlenkamp
Oberst Walter Oesau
Oberst Hans-Ulrich Rudel
Generaladmiral Alfred Saalwachter
Leutnant Adolf Schmahl
SS-Unterscharführer Remi Schrijnen
Hauptmann Rudolf Sigmund
SS-Sturmbannführer Heinrich Springer
Major Ernst Thomsen
Fregattenkapitän Erich Topp
SS-Obersturmbannführer Otto Weidinger
Major Helmut Wick
Oberfeldwebel Walter Wriedt

FOREWORD

It is my special pleasure to write a Foreword to this work.

In France, in 1940, I fought against British soldiers near Hulluch, the Scarpe Canal, on the Somme and at Abbeville, as a Company Commander. It was hard fighting, chivalrous and fair. On this occasion we were in the attack and the British in defence.

In 1944—45, in the defensive battles between the Maas and Rhine, I was a Regimental Commander with 180 Infanterie Division during the withdrawal and rearguard action. Once again the British were our opponents but, this time, they were the attackers and we the defenders.

Today the soldiers of the *Bundeswehr* stand shoulder to shoulder with the British Army, ready to defend the freedom of Europe. During my long service with the *Bundeswehr*, I developed a high regard for the British soldier, determined enemy in war, trusted comrade in peace.

In his book on the Knight's Cross winners of all branches of the German armed forces in World War Two, this British author deserves all our thanks and recognition for his historical appreciation of the German soldier.

> MARTIN STEGLICH
> Oberst a.D.
> Commander 1221 Grenadier Rgt.

Given the opportunity to write a few words towards the Foreword for this book, I would like to dedicate these words to the common soldier. In order to win the Knight's Cross, he had to act solely on his own initiative, striking decisively against the enemy with no thought for his own safety and bringing significant success to his sector of the front.

As a machine-gunner, I was one of these common soldiers, ensnared in the horrific scenery of war. From time to time the common soldier fights with great fatalistic bravery in order to fulfil his duty. Many will fall, believing fully in the justice of their cause, their heroic actions in the heat of battle often unnoticed and unrecorded.

I bear the Knight's Cross in remembrance of these brave men, my Comrades. I am indebted to their sacrifices that I and others might live.

> HANS STURM
> Gefreiter
> Infanterie Regiment 473
> 253 Infanterie Division.

INTRODUCTION

If the Iron Cross of Germany can be considered to be one of the world's best known decorations, then surely the Knight's Cross, the *Ritterkreuz*, must be the best known of all the Iron Crosses. It was introduced to bridge the considerable gap which had existed between the Iron Cross First Class and the Grand Cross of the Iron Cross since the demise of the famed *Pour le Mérite* or 'Blue Max' at the end of World War One.

Virtually from the first award of the Knight's Cross, its recipients were feted as war heroes. Articles and features on Knight's Cross winners, known as *Ritterkreuzträger*, appeared in newspapers and popular magazines of the day. Picture postcards of Knight's Cross winners were printed in large numbers and were avidly collected by an admiring public. Even today, these *Ritterkreuzträger* postcards, especially those by such esteemed war artists as Wolfgang Willrich, are highly sought after by collectors and fetch very high prices. Demand for them has grown to the extent that they are now in fact being reproduced, complete with the appropriate sepia tinting!

The Knight's Cross of the Iron Cross has no direct equivalent in British or American terms. It could be won for a single act of valour in the face of the enemy, in which case it could justifiably be said to be the equivalent of a Victoria Cross. It could also be won by a senior officer for his successful command of a unit during a specific battle or campaign, or over a period of time, when it could be said to equate to the Distinguished Service Order. Equally, many awards of the Knight's Cross to *Luftwaffe* fighter pilots were for continued success in the air war and could be said to be a counterpart of the Distinguished Flying Cross. The Appendices show how the Knight's Cross was distributed amongst the various rank groupings and arms of service, and the numbers awarded during each period of the war. It is hoped that this information will give the reader a better insight into this covetted award and may lay to rest some of the misconceptions which still exist.

Now that over forty years have elapsed since the end of World War Two it is to be hoped that we can look back with a more objective eye and appreciate the acts of valour or distinction for which the various recipients received this decoration. The Knight's Cross of the Iron Cross was a military not a political decoration, and the political beliefs which some of its winners may have held are not relevant to this work. Soldiers of all nations respect bravery in their opponents and appreciate the risks, often with fatal consequences, which the recipient of a high military decoration must undergo. Qualities of leadership are also often held in great admiration. A case in point is General Feldmarschall Erwin Rommel, one of Germany's finest soldiers, whose sense of honour and chivalry as well as his skill and cunning as a commander found him a great deal of respect, not to say admiration, even among his enemies.

ACKNOWLEDGEMENTS

No book of this type can be written without reference to existing printed works, both modern literature and contemporary wartime material. Awards of the Knight's Cross were always well publicised and such original magazines as *Der Adler, Die Wehrmacht, Signal,* etc as well as newspapers such as *Völkischer Beobachter* gave a deal of coverage to the subject of Knight's Cross winners. Since the end of World War Two, two principal works have been written which are the 'Bibles' for anyone carrying out research on this subject: *Die Ritterkreuzträger* by Gerhard von Seemen and *Die Ritterkreuzträger der Waffen-SS* by Ernst Gunther Kratschmer. Both authors were former soldiers of the German armed forces though neither were themselves *Ritterkreuzträger.*

Today, in West Germany, former soldiers of the German Armed Forces who were decorated with the Knight's Cross have their own association, the *Ordensgemeinschaft der Ritterkreuzträger,* which holds regular local meetings as well as a large annual national meeting. Very few works can have been written on the subject of the winners of the Knight's Cross without the assistance of the OdR and its members. This work is no exception.

A large number of veterans, collectors and fellow researchers also contributed their time and material to this project. I am most grateful to them. Pride of place must go to my very good friend Heinrich Springer. Quite simply, without Heinrich's help this book would not exist. Thanks to him I had the pleasure of meeting a number of *Ritterkreuzträger* in person and with his help I was introduced to the OdR and thus made contact with many of the former German soldiers who have contributed to this book. I am happy now to acknowledge his help and encouragement.

The following individuals have also contributed to this book with documentary or photographic material. I gratefully acknowledge their contributions. Chris Ailsby; Friedrich Anding; Ernst Barkmann; Artur Becker-Neetz; Malcolm Bowers; Gerd Bremer; Heinz von Brese; Colin Brown; Hermann Buchner; Josef Charita; Arthur Charlton; Brian L Davis; Rolf Dûe; Max Fabich; Johann Fiedler; Heinrich Gath; Otto Giese; Günther Goebel; Peter Groch; Martin Gross; Heinz-Günther Guderian; Heinz-Martin Hadeball; Hermann Haderecker; Reinhard Hardegen; Willi Hein; Willi Heinrich; Heinz Heuer; Peter Huckstepp; Helmut Hudel; Herbert Ihlefeld; Bruno Kahl; Gerhard Konopka; Ernst-August Krag; Siegfried Keiling; Hans Lex; David Littlejohn; Heinz Macher; Johannes Mühlenkamp; Karl-Heinz Oesterwitz; Pete Pleetinik; Johann Pongratz; Josef-Wilhelm Rettemeier; Daniel Rose; Hans Sandrock; Dr Erich Schroedter; Karl-Heinz Schulz-Lepel; Richard Schulze-Kossens; Jak P Mallmann Showell; Franz Siebert; Alfred Siegling; Martin Steglich; Fred Stephens; Hans Sturm; Ernst Heinrich Thomsen; Gerhard Tschierschwitz; Alexander Uhlig; the staff of the US Document Centre, Berlin; Otto Weidinger; Walter von Wietersheim; Theodor Wisch; Günther Wisliceny.

THE KNIGHT'S CROSS
OF THE IRON CROSS

The Knight's Cross of the Iron Cross was instituted on 1 September 1939 at the same time as the re-institution of the Iron Cross itself. The institution document reads as follows:

After I have determined to call to arms the German people, as a defence against an attack that threatens them, in memory of the sons of Germany who in heroic battles in the previous great wars have stood for the country, I renew the Order of the Iron Cross.

ARTICLE 1
The Iron Cross will be awarded in the following classes:
   Iron Cross Second Class
   Iron Cross First Class
   Knight's Cross of the Iron Cross
   Grand Cross of the Iron Cross

ARTICLE 2
  i. The Iron Cross will be awarded for outstanding service to service personnel and for bravery in the face of the enemy.
 ii. The Cross for a higher class must be preceded by that of a lower class.

ARTICLE 3
The awarding of the Grand Cross depends on my own decision for outstanding deeds which are decisive. Articles 1 and 4 state that the Iron Cross has the following classes and is awarded in the following order: Second Class, First Class, Knight's Cross and Grand Cross.

ARTICLE 4
  i. The Iron Cross First and Second Class are the same as for those in World War One except that there is on the face a swastika and the date 1939. The reverse of the Second Class has the year 1813. The Second Class is worn on a black, white and red ribbon on a medal bar or in the buttonhole. The First Class is worn without a ribbon on the left breast.
 ii. The Knight's Cross is larger than the Iron Cross Second Class. It is worn on a black white and red ribbon around the neck.
iii. The Grand Cross is twice the size of the Iron Cross Second Class and is worn on a wide black white and red ribbon around the neck.

ARTICLE 5
The holder of either class of the Iron Cross of World War One who distinguishes himself will receive a silver clasp with an eagle (wings outspread) holding a wreath and swastika and the year 1939 which will be worn on the ribbon in the case of the Second Class and pinned above the Cross on the left breast in the case of the First Class.

ARTICLE 6
The award will be accompanied by a possession certificate.

ARTICLE 7
The Iron Cross in the case of death will be returned to the next of kin at the family home.

ARTICLE 8
The Headquarters of the Chief of the Army High Command, Reichsminister with the Minister of State and Chief of the Presiding Council.

Berlin, 1 September 1939
Der Führer (*Hitler*)
Chief of the Army High Command (*Keitel*)

Reichsminister of the Interior (*Frick*)
Minister of State (*Meissner*)

The Knight's Cross was the natural successor to the Imperial *Pour le Mérite* and in the tradition of that earlier award, was to be worn around the neck *am Halse*.

Strangely, although this decoration was to be known as the Knight's Cross, or *Ritterkreuz*, Hitler had strong views on the Prussian concept of honour and chivalry, seeing it as outdated and bourgeois. Note that the German title *Ritterkreuzträger* translates as 'Knight's Cross bearer', almost as if the decoration was somewhat of a burden. Indeed, it is known that many senior German officers had strong feelings over this and felt that the title should be changed to *Ritter des Eisernen Kreuzes* — 'Knight of the Iron Cross'. This would of course be a much more accurate description for a winner of the Knight's grade of an Order.

An approach *was* made on this subject, to Generaloberst Jodl in 1944, in the hope that he might influence Hitler on the matter. Jodl, however, knowing full well Hitler's attitude towards the subject refused even to raise the matter.

THE KNIGHT'S CROSS DESCRIBED

The 1939 Knight's Cross of the Iron Cross consisted of a cast iron centre which bore on the face a swastika in the centre and the date of institution 1939 in the lower arm. The reverse featured only the date of the original institution of the Iron Cross, 1813. The entire centre was finished in a matt or semi-matt black, with the swastika and dates often polished to a sheen.

The centre was held within a two-part silver frame featuring a beaded inner edge and a smooth outer edge. The beaded edge was finished in matt white silver oxide whilst the outer edge was burnished to a mirror finish, a very attractive contrast. In almost every case, the swastika in the centre is level with the height of the beaded edge, whereas on many spurious post war copies, the swastika is much lower.

In the centre of the upper arm was a small eyelet through which the ribbon loop passed. On the reverse of the upper arm of the frame there was a small silver content mark, 800, indicating 800 parts per 1000 purity. The ribbon loop, consisting of an oval coil of silver wire, was also usually hallmarked with the '800' silver content mark. Normally, only the silver content mark is found on the Knight's Cross, makers marks being only rarely encountered. The one which does occur most often, however, is that of the esteemed Berlin firm of C E Juncker, whose code number was L/12. The overall size of the decoration was usually 48mm × 55mm.

The Knight's Cross was presented in a small rectangular case measuring

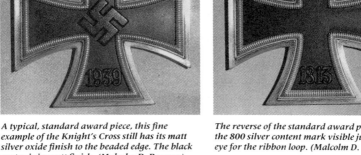

A typical, standard award piece, this fine example of the Knight's Cross still has its matt silver oxide finish to the beaded edge. The black centre is in matt finish. (Malcolm D. Bowers.)

The reverse of the standard award piece, with the 800 silver content mark visible just below the eye for the ribbon loop. (Malcolm D. Bowers.)

A superb, high quality example of the Knight's Cross by the firm of C. E. Juncker of Berlin, in its original presentation case. (Peter Huckstepp.)

The reverse of the C. E. Juncker Knight's Cross. The paintwork on this example is smoother than the previous piece and has a slight sheen. (Peter Huckstepp.)

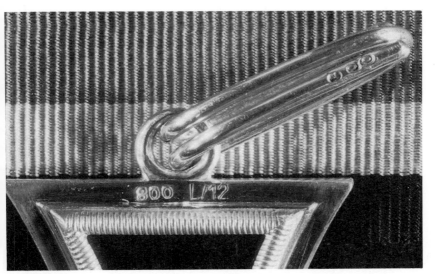

A close up of the various markings on the
Juncker Knight's Cross. Next to the 800 silver
content mark is the L/12 maker's mark of the
Juncker firm. The silver content mark also
appears on the ribbon loop. (Peter Huckstepp.)

155mm × 85mm × 27mm. The outer surface was covered in black simulated leather devoid of any motif. The lid interior was finished in padded white satin or silk, whilst the base was covered in black velvet, and was fitted to accept the shape of the award. A recess was also provided for the ribbon. The case was fastened by a small spring clip.

The ribbon for the Knight's Cross was in the same colours and proportions as that for the Iron Cross Second Class, but it was wider, 45mm. The ribbon was fastened around the neck by a variety of methods, including press studs, tie strings and elastic, but as the ribbon was almost totally obscured by the collar, the method of attachment was largely academic.

Miniatures of the Knight's Cross are also known. These could be in the form of stick pins, or could be exact miniatures complete with miniature ribbon, usually bowed, and designed to be worn at the buttonhole of civilian clothes.

VARIANTS

Very few true variants of the Knight's Cross were ever produced as only a small number of firms were authorised to manufacture them and quality control was very strict. A few original specimens with the 'low' swastika referred to elsewhere have been encountered as has been a version with the eyelet for the ribbon loop indented into the rim rather than sitting atop the edge. The principal differences usually encountered, however, are in the materials.

Original officially awarded pieces were manufactured with an iron centre

13

An unusual presentation case for the Knight's Cross presented to General Böhme by the 7 Gebirgs Division. The bronzed octagonal casket is topped by a Gebirgsjäger mountain boot. (Pierre Pleetinik via Frederick J Stephens.)

Visible on the interior of the casket lid is the number, 7, of the Gebirgs Division; on the base is a plate giving details of the presentation. (Pierre Pleetinik via Frederick J Stephens.)

The interior of the casket has a recessed base, fitted to the shape of the Knight's Cross. There is no facility for a ribbon to be contained within the casket. (Pierre Pleetinik.)

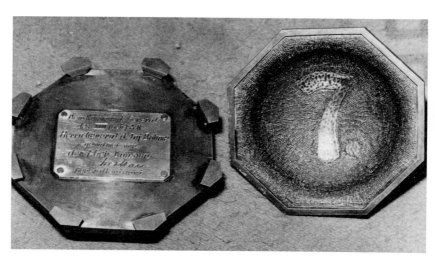

A typical method of wear for the Knight's Cross was the use of elastic stitched to the ribbon. As this was concealed under the tunic or shirt collar, it was not visible anyway and, in fact, any suitable method could be used. This particular Cross was won by **Luftwaffe** night fighter ace Hauptmann Rudolf Sigmund. (Daniel Rose.)

An Iron Cross Second Class converted for use as a Knight's Cross. The ribbon ring has been removed and a smaller ring to take the ribbon loop added. Otherwise, the Cross is unaltered. (A. E. Prowse.)

and a genuine silver rim. Many *Ritterkreuzträger*, however, purchased additional Crosses at their own expense and these pieces could be in a range of materials, including copper and zinc for the centres and silver-plated white metal, brass and various grades of genuine silver for the rim.

Collectors may occasionally encounter a specimen which bears the '800' silver mark and yet is clearly some other metal silver-plated. This does not necessarily indicate it is a reproduction. Continental hallmarking practices permit the use of silver marks on such pieces, indicating the grade of silver used in the plating!

15

The 1957 'de-Nazified' version of the Knight's Cross with the swastika centre replaced by a sprig of Oakleaves. The design of the Swords and Oakleaves remains unchanged. (Author Collection.)

The reverse face of the 1957 Swords and Oakleaves is just visible in this shot and the plain undetailed reverse of the Swords is evident. Examples with the reverse detailed, as on wartime award pieces, are not currently made except as reproductions. (Author Collection.)

Knight's Crosses made 'in the field' should also be considered. Often, in the case of awards to U-boat Captains for example, a wait of several weeks might ensue after notification of the award before the U-boat reached port and the award ceremony could take place. In many such cases, the mechanics in the crew would manufacture a replica of the award and make a shipboard presentation. Many such Crosses would be worn even after the official award because of the sentimental value of the replica Cross to a popular Captain.

Finally, it may be worth noting that many Iron Crosses Second Class were converted into Knight's Crosses for wear in the field or because no genuine pieces were available at the time of the award ceremony where this was 'in the Field'. Generally, these conversions were merely a matter of removing the Second Class ribbon ring and adding a Knight's Cross style loop.

THE KNIGHT'S CROSS AWARD DOCUMENTS

When an award of the Knight's Cross was made, the recipient's Commanding Officer would be notified by telegram that Hitler had approved the award. The Commanding Officer of the recipient's unit or the Commander of its parent unit would receive a typed Preliminary Certificate or *Vorläufiges Besitzzeugnis* and present this to the new *Ritterkreuzträger*.

This Preliminary Certificate was a simple printed document bearing

VORLÄUFIGES BESITZZEUGNIS at the centre top, followed by a small Iron Cross motif, then:

Der Führer
und Oberste Befehlshaber
der Wehrmacht, hat dem...[recipient's name, rank and unit]...
das Ritterkreuz
des Eisernen Kreuzes
am...[date]...*verliehen.*

Then followed the signature of the senior officer confirming the award. Among signatures encountered are von Brauchitsch, Keitel, and Burgdorf. At the bottom left corner of the document is the rubber stamp mark of the awarding authority.

This type of Preliminary Certificate is known in two forms, with Latin or Gothic letter types. Later in the war, a new style of Certificate was introduced, often found with the details typed on with a typewriter using a particularly large typeface. After the Iron Cross motif followed the legend:

Der Führer
Hat Dem
...[details of recipient]...
Das Ritterkreuz
Des Eisernen Kreuzes
Am...[date]...*Verliehen*

It was originally intended that each recipient would be presented with a large, formal *Urkunde* and Hitler assembled a team of the finest artisans to produce these magnificent pieces. This *Urkunde* consisted of a large 700mm × 430mm parchment vellum sheet folded in half to produce four pages. The facing page was hand-lettered.

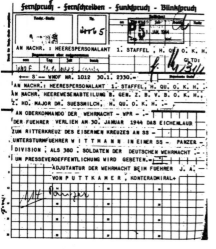

Typical example of a telegram giving initial notification of an award, in this case the Oakleaves. In this case, the telegram originated with one of Hitler's adjutants, Konteradmiral von Puttkamer. This telegram would precede the **Vorläufiges Besitzzeugnis** *and, ultimately, in many cases, the elaborate* **Urkunde.** *(USDC)*

At the top centre was a large national emblem, the Eagle and Swastika, over the legend:

Im Namen
Des Deutschen Volkes
Verleihe Ich
Dem...**[rank of recipient]**...
[name of recipient]
Das Ritterkreuz
Des Eisernen Kreuzes
[next came a small Iron Cross motif]
Führerhauptquartier
Den...**[date]**...
Der Führer
Und Oberste Befehlshaber
Der Wehrmacht.

At the bottom of the page was the signature of Adolf Hitler. Apart from the recipient's name which was hand-lettered in gold leaf and Hitler's signature, the whole design was executed in red brown ink.

This elaborate document was contained in a leather folder lined with parchment. The face of the folder was embossed with a large eagle and

*Standard **Verläufiges Besitzzeugnis** from the first half of the war. The layout and wording was standardised and little or no variation will be encountered. This particular certificate was presented to night fighter ace Rudolf Sigmund. (Daniel Rose.)*

*Variant to the standard **Voläufiges Besitzzeugnis**. This version has the text in Gothic script but is in all other ways identical to the normal pattern. (Chris Ailsby.)*

VORLÄUFIGES BESITZZEUGNIS

DER FÜHRER
HAT DEM
SS-Unterscharführer B a r k m a n n ,
4./ SS-Pz.Rgt. 2

DAS RITTERKREUZ
DES EISERNEN KREUZES
AM 27.8.1944 VERLIEHEN

HQu OKH. DEN 5.September 1944

OBERKOMMANDO DES HEERES
I.A.

GENERALLEUTNANT

The form of **Vorläufiges Besitzzeugnis** commonly issued after the mid-war period. This particular certificate was awarded to Panzer ace, Ernst Barkmann. The signature is that of Generalleutnant Burgdorf. (Ernst Barkmann).

The exterior of the binder for the Diamonds. The outer face is in leather with a gilt metal geometric pattern border and gilt metal eagle with diamond studded swastika. (Chris Ailsby/Hans-Ulrich Rudel.)

The elaborate **Urkunde** for the Knight's Cross, the entire design executed in red-brown ink with the exception of the recipient's name which is in gold. (Forman Piccadilly.)

The **Urkunde** for the Diamonds is basically identical in design to that for the Knight's Cross but the wording is altered to suit. In this case, the entire text is executed in gold. (Chris Ailsby/Hans-Ulrich Rudel.)

IM NAMEN
DES DEUTSCHEN VOLKES
VERLEIHE ICH
DEM GENERALMAJOR
GERHARD BERTHOLD
DAS RITTERKREUZ
DES EISERNEN KREUZES

FÜHRERHAUPTQUARTIER
DEN 4. DEZEMBER 1941
DER FÜHRER
UND OBERSTE BEFEHLSHABER
DER WEHRMACHT

IM NAMEN
DES DEUTSCHEN VOLKES
VERLEIHE ICH
DEM MAJOR
HANS ULLRICH RUDEL
DAS EICHENLAUB MIT
SCHWERTERN UND BRILLANTEN
ZUM RITTERKREUZ
DES EISERNEN KREUZES

FÜHRERHAUPTQUARTIER
DEN 29. MÄRZ 1944
DER FÜHRER
UND OBERSTE BEFEHLSHABER
DER WEHRMACHT

swastika in gold leaf. Just inside the rear cover was the name of the binder, Frieda Thiersch, in gold leaf.

It was originally intended that recipients of Generalfeldmarschall rank would receive a more elaborate folder bearing a complex gilt geometrical patterning around the border of the face. This type is illustrated in the original wartime publication *Die Kunst Im Dritten Reich*, (October 1942 issue). It is not known, however, if this type was actually used.

Due to wartime conditions and the large number of folders which would have been required, only a limited number of *Ritterkreuzträger* received the *Urkunde*. It has been suggested that only those who received the Knight's Cross personally from Hitler were given the *Urkunde*. This was not the case. One friend of the author, former Waffen-SS Sturmbannführer Heinrich Springer, whose war experiences are described elsewhere in this book, never received a *Vorläufiges Besitzzeugnis*, but whilst recovering from his wounds in hospital after the action in which his award was earned, he was visited by his Divisional Commander Josef 'Sepp' Dietrich and presented with the *Urkunde*.

Both the *Vorläufiges Besitzzeugnis* and the *Urkunde* are extremely rare and are highly sought after by collectors. Hence, the value of these items is very high and this has led to some very expert forgeries appearing.

THE OAKLEAVES

The Oakleaves to the Knight's Cross of the Iron Cross were instituted on 3 June 1940 and were intended to recognise further meritorious action after the award of the Knight's Cross.

The Oakleaves clasp consisted of a spray of three oakleaves with the central

Reverse view of a set of Oakleaves showing the silver content mark 800 on the left and the maker's code 11 to the right. This maker's mark is rather uncommon. (Peter Groch.)

The Oakleaves to the Knight's Cross, shown to advantage in the original black velvet lined presentation case. The exterior of the lid is plain black without any motif on the standard case. This particular piece has the LDO logo. (John Shaw.)

A variant set of Oakleaves. This piece lacks the normal concave effect and carries the silver content number 900. (Chris Ailsby.)

Variation set of Oakleaves. This set bears no silver content mark and is therefore probably only silver plated. It is otherwise identical to the standard Oakleaves and has the usual concave effect to the reverse. (Author Collection.)

A variant high quality set of Oakleaves in 900 silver. (Chris Ailsby.)

leaf overlapping the lower two. The rib of the central leaf was in the form of a highly stylised letter 'L'. This was an inherited feature of the Oakleaves clasps of earlier Imperial German Decorations and is said to commemorate Queen Louise the wife of King Friedrich Wilhelm, institutor of the original Iron Cross in 1813.

The Oakleaves clasp measures 20mm × 20mm and was struck in solid silver. The reverse was slightly concave with a replacement loop welded to the centre. The silver content mark was usually stamped on the reverse and ranged from 800 to 990, with 900 being the commonest on actual awarded pieces. Makers code numbers can also be encountered on the reverse, with L/12 and 21 being those most often found. Occasional pieces in silvered brass can also be

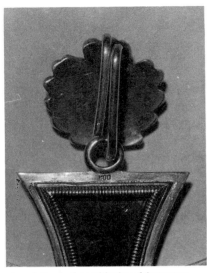

The reverse of this set of Oakleaves has the 800 silver content mark set vertically on the left hand side of the reverse face. Note also the 800 silver mark on the Cross itself. (T. J. Stannard.)

A variation in the positioning of the content mark, this example has the 800 stamped horizontally in the bottom right hand corner of the reverse face of the Oakleaves. (Chris Ailsby.)

A standard set of Oakleaves shown as worn on the Knight's Cross. (Malcolm D. Bowers.)

This photograph shows a privately-purchased additional Knight's Cross. The Cross itself is stamped 935 and the Oakleaves are stamped 800, horizontally on the centre left reverse face. (Malcolm D. Bowers.)

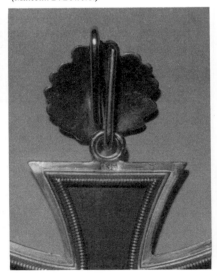

encountered. These are not award pieces but additional specimens obtained by recipients at their own expense.

The Oakleaves were awarded in a black case measuring 100mm × 75mm × 25mm lined with padded white silk to the lid and black velvet to the base.

The *Vorläufiges Besitzzeugnis* for the Oakleaves was very similar to that for the Knight's Cross, but with the text altered to read *Das Eichenlaub zum Ritterkreuz*. The lettering to the *Urkunde* was similarly altered and also had the national emblem executed in gold leaf rather than red ink. The binder was in white leather with the national emblem on the cover in gilt metal.

THE SWORDS AND OAKLEAVES

Instituted on 15 July 1941, the Swords were a traditional German device and may be found on a number of German decorations. The Swords to the Knight's Cross consisted of two crossed swords at an angle of 40 degrees with the right hand blade uppermost. The overall size was 25mm × 10mm. These Swords were welded to the base of a replacement set of Oakleaves and were never awarded on their own. The official award pieces were detailed on both obverse and reverse faces, although the Oakleaves remained blank on the reverse. The maker's mark and silver content mark are usually found on the reverse of the Oakleaves. The word SILBER is also occasionally found on the reverse of the Oakleaves.

Variants exist with the reverse of the Swords blank. These came in a variety

The Swords and Oakleaves. On this private purchase set, the ball ends of the crossguards contact the opposing blades. This feature is not found on the actual award pieces. (Chris Ailsby.)

Reverse of the private-purchase Swords and Oakleaves. The reverse face of the Swords is undetailed. (Chris Ailsby.)

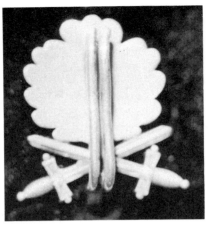

Reverse of an original issue set of Oakleaves and Swords. The Swords are fully detailed on the reverse face. (Colin Brown.)

An unusual variation of the Oakleaves and Swords. Compare the large size of the Swords and the angle at which they cross with the normal type. This particular piece does not carry any silver content marks and appears to be silver plated. (David Littlejohn.)

of materials from plated brass to 990 silver and are additional pieces obtained at the wearer's expense.

With regard to these additional pieces it should be noted that although initially some *Ritterkreuzträger* purchased these through retail outlets, it is known that this practice was officially prohibited and all requests for additional sets were to be made through the Orders Commission. It is debatable, however, if this ban on retail sales was adhered to strictly.

The *Vorläufiges Besitzzeugnis* and *Urkunde* were once again similar to those for the Knight's Cross with the wording appropriately altered to read *'Das Eichenlaub Mit Schwertern Zum Ritterkreuz Des Eisernen Kreuzes'*. The folder for the *Urkunde* had the addition of a gilt metal geometric border.

THE SWORDS, OAKLEAVES AND DIAMONDS

Instituted on 15 July 1941, the Diamonds consisted of a hand-crafted set of silver Oakleaves and Swords set with numerous small diamonds. According to Dr Klietmann, however, sets issued in 1941−42 were in silver whereas those issued after 1942 were in platinum. Unlike the standard Oakleaves and Swords, the Oakleaves on these pieces were hollow to allow for better light reflection through the stones. As they were jeweller-made individual pieces, no two are exactly identical and the number and position of the stones may vary considerably from piece to piece. Some pieces feature diamonds on the Oakleaves only, whilst others have the Sword hilts set with stones also.

A fine example of the beautiful Swords, Oakleaves and Diamonds. Note the more oval shape of the Oakleaves when compared to the normal set. (Josef Charita.)

A variation of the Swords, Oakleaves and Diamonds, based on the standard Oakleaves and Swords. Once again, on this variation set, the ball ends to the crossguards touch the opposing blades. (Josef Charita.)

Recipients received two sets, one with genuine diamonds, the other for everyday use with imitation stones. The contemporary copies obtained as extra sets by Diamonds winners were usually solid silver types as per the ordinary Swords and Oakleaves, as opposed to the hollow award pieces. The reverse on this type would normally carry the silver content mark.

The award documents for the Diamonds were as for the previous grades with the wording suitably altered and in the case of the *Urkunde*, the entire text executed in gold leaf. The leather cover for the binder was in a colour to suit the arm of service of the recipient: red-brown for the army and *Waffen-SS*, dark blue for the navy and grey blue for the *Luftwaffe*. On some examples, the swastika on the metal national emblem on the cover is set with small diamonds.

THE GOLDEN SWORDS, OAKLEAVES AND DIAMONDS

This award, instituted on 29 December 1944, was intended to have been awarded to a maximum of only twelve of the country's bravest soldiers. However, only one was ever awarded, to the famed *Stuka* pilot Oberst Hans-Ulrich Rudel.

The award consists of a set of Swords and Oakleaves worked in 18 carat gold and set with 50 diamonds. It was produced by the old established Berlin jewellers firm of Godet, though the pieces were not maker marked. As far as can be ascertained, no special documents were produced for this award.

The actual Golden Oakleaves, Swords and Diamonds won by Stuka ace Oberst Hans-Ulrich Rudel. This set remained in the possession of Oberst Rudel after the war. (Chris Ailsby/Hans-Ulrich Rudel.)

Oberst Rudel, the sole recipient of the Golden Oakleaves, Swords and Diamonds shown here wearing the award, whilst on the Eastern Front. Rudel also wears the Pilot/Observer's Badge with Diamonds and the Gold Flight Clasp with Diamonds. (Chris Ailsby/Hans-Ulrich Rudel.)

THE GERMAN CROSS IN GOLD

The reader will find this award mentioned numerous times throughout this book, and will note that it is worn by most of the Knight's Cross winners in the photographs. Whilst it is not part of the history of the Knight's Cross, it is an important enough award to warrant description here.

The German Cross was instituted on 28 September 1941 and was intended to bridge the considerable gap which existed between the Iron Cross First Class and the Knight's Cross, much in the same way that the Knight's Cross itself was introduced to bridge the gap between the Iron Cross First Class and the Grand Cross. It was designed by Professor Dr Klein of Munich and was first produced by the firm of Deschler und Sohn in that city.

The award consists of a large sunburst star, 63mm in diameter, struck in bronze or tombak with a silvered finish, the highpoint of each ray of the sunburst being burnished. On top of this star was laid an identical star which was marginally smaller and finished in a very dark grey. This gave the impression of a dark star with a silver border. In the centre of the star was a matt silver disc surrounded by a gilt wreath of laurel leaves bearing the date of institution '1941' at the base. In the centre of the disc was a black-enamelled, silver-edged swastika. The swastika is in fact the 'German Cross' of the title. The whole

26

Obverse of the German Cross. Both grades were identical, only the colour of the central laurel wreath differed.

Reverse of the German Cross. Small rivets were used to assemble the multi-part award. Examples are encountered with four or six rivets of either the solid or hollow type. (Author Collection.)

Cloth-embroidered version of the German Cross in Gold. The metal wreath from the standard version is used. The example illustrated is on black cloth backing indicating its intended use on the black Panzer uniform. (Author Collection.)

assembly is rivetted together and on the plain, slightly concave reverse of the outer star was a large wide, flat hinged pin for attachment of the award to the right breast of the uniform.

The German Cross was awarded in a square black case lined with white padded satin to the lid and black velvet or flock to the base. There is no motif to be found on the lid of this case, but a small gold edge line for the Gold award and a silver edge for the Silver award.

The German Cross was also manufactured in a cloth embroidered 'active service' version which could be stitched directly to the uniform. Photographic evidence suggests that this type saw fairly widespread use, unlike cloth versions of the Iron Cross which were rarely ever worn. The dimensions of the cloth versions were identical to that for the metal type. Although a few all fabric versions are known, most of the cloth types made use of the metal laurel wreath from the standard version. The colour of backing cloth varied depending on the branch of service of the wearer, and included Field Grey, grey-blue, navy blue, black, etc.

As with the Knight's Cross, the German Cross was accompanied by a *Vorläufiges Besitzzeugnis*, followed by an *Urkunde* in some but not all cases. The *Urkunde* would normally be signed by the Commander-in-Chief of the service to which the winner belonged. In the case of the army, this would be von Brauchitsch or Keitel, for the navy, Grossadmiral Dönitz or Raeder and for the *Luftwaffe*, Reichsmarschall Göring.

It should be emphasised that the German Cross was not part of the Iron Cross series of awards. It was, however, common practice, after the institution of this award, that the German Cross would be awarded after the Iron Cross First Class and before the Knight's Cross. While it *was* necessary for a recipient already to hold the Iron Cross First Class, it was *not* a prerequisite for the award of the Knight's Cross that the recipient should hold the German Cross. There are several examples of awards of the German Cross being made long after the award of the Knight's Cross and, equally, many examples of Knight's Cross winners who never received a German Cross.

The erroneous idea that the German Cross was part of the Iron Cross series of awards was further perpetuated in 1957 with the introduction of the 'denazified' versions of the wartime decorations. The 'new' German Cross has the swastika replaced by a small Iron Cross motif. The silver version, which in its wartime form, differed only in the colour of the laurel wreath, now has a small War Merit Cross motif, thus changing its appearance quite considerably.

The number of German Crosses awarded from its institution in 1941 until the end of the war was approximately 16,800 to the army and *Waffen-SS*, 1300 to the navy, and just under 7000 to the *Luftwaffe*.

Distribution of the German Cross amongst the various rank gradings shown below in approximate percentages makes an interesting comparison with the percentages shown for the Knight's Cross.

Rank	Percentage
Generals and General Staff Officers	5
Colonels and Lieutenant Colonels	10
Majors	11
Captains	22
Lieutenants	33
Non Commissioned Ranks	17
Other Ranks	2

Like the Knight's Cross, the value of original examples of the German Cross has risen quite dramatically over the past few years. At the time of writing, a genuine German Cross in Gold with its original case, once available for around £20, is fetching well in excess of £400. Unfortunately, the rise in value has also meant an increase in the number of reproduction pieces in circulation. Fortunately, however, the complexity of construction of the original piece and the cost of this process has meant that few reproductions can stand comparison with a genuine piece and so can usually be detected quite quickly.

1939
THE BLITZKRIEG

September 1939 saw the German invasion of Poland in a campaign so swift that it left the world stunned at the lightning speed of the German advance and the new tactics of armoured warfare. For the first time, an army was going to war with what looked like almost perfect co-ordination and co-operation between the various branches of the armed forces. Although the *Wehrmacht* was ultimately to suffer much inter-service rivalry, in 1939 it seemed invincible as it swept aside all opposition and stormed on to victory after victory.

There were no doubt many examples of great gallantry on both sides as the plucky Poles fought desperately for every inch of their homeland. However, as might be expected with a new decoration where no previous awards existed to give precedents for the suitability of recipients, very few Knight's Crosses were awarded during the Polish Campaign. The first batch of awards of the Knight's Cross, on 30 September 1939, were without exception to high ranking officers for their successful command of the conquering German armies. The first ten awards were as follows:

Generaloberst Johannes Blaskowitz, Commander 8 Army
Generaloberst Walter von Brauchitsch, Commander-in-Chief Army
Generalfeldmarschall Hermann Göring, Commander-in-Chief *Luftwaffe*
General der Flieger Albert Kesselring, Commander 1 Air Fleet
General der Artillerie Georg von Küchler, Commander 3 Army
Generaloberst Wilhelm List, Commander 14 Army
General der Flieger Alexander Löhr, Commander 4 Air Fleet
Grossadmiral Erich Raeder, Commander-in-Chief Navy
General der Artillerie Walther von Reichenau, Commander 10 Army
Generaloberst Gerd von Rundstedt, Commander-in-Chief Army Group South

The first award of a Knight's Cross for an individual action was to Kapitänleutnant Gunther Prien, Commander of *U-47*, for the successful penetration of the Royal Navy anchorage at Scapa Flow in the Orkneys and the destruction there of the battleship HMS *Royal Oak*. Even this, however, could be construed as a leadership award as, of course, the entire crew had taken part in the operation, not just Prien. This was, in fact, recognised by the award of a decoration to every member of the crew.

The second large batch of awards was made on 27 October when eleven Knight's Crosses were awarded, as follows:

Generalleutnant Kurt von Briesen, Commander 30 Infanterie Division
General der Panzertruppe Heinz Guderian, Commanding General XIX Armee Korps
General der Artillerie Franz Halder, Chief of the General Staff
General der Kavallerie Erich Hoepner, Commanding General XVI Armee Korps
General der Infanterie Hermann Hoth, Commanding General XV Armee Korps

Generalmajor Ludwig Kühler, Commander 1 Gebirgs Division
Generalleutnant Friedrich Olbricht, Commander 24 Infanterie Division
Oberst August Schmidt, Commander Infanterie Regiment 20
Hauptmann Dietrich Steinhardt, Commander 2 Bataillon, Infanterie Regt 20
Leutnant Josef Stolz, Platoon Commander 10/Infanterie Regt 51
General der Infanterie Adolf Strauss, Commanding General II Armee Korps

So, by the end of 1939, when the Polish Campaign had been successfully
concluded and the Germans began to prepare to launch the assault in the
West, only four out of the 22 Knight's Crosses awarded were to ranks less than
general. The awards of the Knight's Cross at this time, in fact, closely paralleled
the awards of the Grand Cross in earlier wars.

KAPITÄNLEUTNANT GÜNTHER PRIEN

Günther Prien was born in Osterfeld in January 1908 and joined the *Reichs-marine* in 1933. After his initial training as a U-boat man, and his commissioning as a Leutnant zur See, he was posted to *U-26* as Watchkeeping Officer. In 1938, he returned to U-boat training school and after his course of instruction, was given command of his own vessel, *U-47*. Prien was a born sailor who loved every minute at sea. He admitted to his comrades that he got much more enjoyment from training exercises than he ever got from going on leave.

Prien's superiors were greatly impressed by his attitude to his job and his clear-thinking responses to problems. When Admiral Dönitz, the Commander-in-Chief U-Boats, drew up his plan to attack the British Navy's fleet anchorage at Scapa Flow, Prien was high on the list of potential candidates for the mission. When confronted with the plan, Prien was given time to think it over but knew within himself straight away that he would accept, even though many considered it little more than a suicide mission.

In reality, however, the defences at Scapa Flow were not as effective as either the Germans or the British had thought and Prien succeeded in entering the anchorage undetected. It was an impressive feat of seamanship and Prien's success was crowned when he sank the battleship HMS *Royal Oak* and then escaped unscathed in the panic which ensued. The British could hardly believe that a U-boat could so easily enter Scapa Flow and sink a major warship, then escape — so much so that rumours of German spies and sabotage were soon rife. Indeed, some sources find Prien's success hard to believe even today and the sabotage stories still abound. Winston Churchill, however, admitted to Prien's great success when he told Parliament:

When we consider that during the whole course of the last war this anchorage was found to be immune from such attacks on account of the obstacles imposed by the currents and the net barrages, this entry by a U-boat must be considered as a remarkable feat of professional skill and daring.

Kapitänleutnant Günther Prien, shown here on the conning tower of U-47. He wears the traditional white topped cap of the U-boat Commander and the leather jacket commonly worn by U-boat crew members. (Author Collection.)

Prien receives his Knight's Cross at an investiture at the Reichskanzlei. Here, he shakes hands with Hitler whilst a smiling Grossadmiral Erich Raeder stands in the background. (F. J. Stephen.)

31

The Germans were of course jubilant at this phenomenal propaganda success. Hitler summoned the entire crew to Berlin where every member of the crew was decorated, Prien receiving the Knight's Cross from Hitler personally. The official date of Prien's award was 18 October 1939. Prien's subsequent career was equally successful, with the Oakleaves being awarded almost exactly one year to the day after his Knight's Cross. Prien was the first U-boat Commander to reach a score of 200,000 tons of enemy shipping sunk. On 7 March 1941, however, Prien's luck ran out when *U-47* was attacked and sunk by HMS *Wolverine*. All hands were lost. Prien's score at his time of death was 213,000 tons, representing 32 enemy ships. Had he survived, he may well have become the war's greatest U-boat 'ace'.

Admiral Dönitz himself composed the obituary notice for Prien, and the following tribute appeared in the newspaper *Völkischer Beobachter* (*People's Observer*):

The hero of Scapa Flow has made his last cruise. Although the ocean covers him, Gunther Prien will remain forever amongst us. We have lost him, but we have won him again for he will for all eternity be the model for submarine warfare.

1940
THE CAMPAIGN IN THE WEST

The year 1940 started quietly for the Third Reich. January saw some minor actions against Allied shipping by Dönitz's U-boats and by *Luftwaffe* bombers. The following month found the *Kriegsmarine* flexing its muscles once again as the battlecruisers *Scharnhorst* and *Gneisenau* put to sea. Although their cruise was not exactly an overwhelming success, their escorting U-boats were able to sink twelve merchantmen and one destroyer from the Allied convoys which the battlecruisers sought.

During March, the 'Phoney War' continued, with a number of minor sorties by both sides. The Royal Air Force contented itself with dropping propaganda leaflets whilst Göring's *Luftwaffe* carried out an unsuccessful raid on Scapa Flow, seeking to emulate Prien's success.

The first major campaign of the year came in April when the Germans launched Operation *WESERUBUNG*, split into two phases, *NORD* and *SUD*, the former being the invasion of Norway and the latter the occupation of Denmark. Whereas the Danes quickly gave up the unequal struggle, realising that they could never hope successfully to defend their small country against the might of the *Wehrmacht*, the Norwegians were made of sterner stuff and fought back stubbornly and occasionally with great success, such as the sinking of the heavy cruiser *Blucher* by Norwegian shore batteries. British warships scored great successes over the German naval forces at Narvik, while the Cruiser *Königsberg* was sunk by the Fleet Air Arm at Bergen. On land, British and French ground forces fought tenaciously alongside their Norwegian allies.

On 10 May, the German *Blitzkrieg* was unleashed upon Holland, Belgium and Luxembourg. Over 70 army divisions and in excess of 3500 aircraft struck westwards. Three Panzer Korps smashed through Belgium and Luxembourg as the Anglo-French forces advanced to meet them. The *Luftwaffe* had destroyed vast numbers of Allied aircraft on the ground and, in any case, many of the Allied aircraft types were obsolescent and no match for the *Luftwaffe*'s latest models. Whilst the Allies fought back bravely, they were steadily pushed back through France and over the River Meuse. Meanwhile, the *Luftwaffe* had bombed Rotterdam into submission and Holland had surrendered.

Lightning fast thrusts by Guderian's Panzers were halted just short of Dunkirk, thus allowing a large part of the British Expeditionary Force and many French troops to be evacuated to England. By the time the German advance into Dunkirk continued, over 330,000 men had been rescued. Around 40,000 stragglers were captured. The German advance then turned south into the heart of France, capturing the remnants of the French IX Corps and the British 51 Highland Division at St Valery en Caux on 12 June, just three days after the victorious conclusion of the campaign in Norway. Hitler had had every reason to be pleased with the result of the Norwegian battles. The German commander in Norway, General Dietl, had admitted that by the time the Allied

Hauptmann Johann Pongratz was awarded the Knight's Cross as an Oberfeldwebel with Infanterie Regiment 74 in September 1940. (Johann Pongratz)

General der Infanterie Hans Jordan, shown here as an Oberst, won the Knight's Cross in June 1940 during the French Campaign, the Oakleaves in January 1942 on the Eastern Front and the Swords in April 1944. Notice the cloth covers worn to disguise the unit numbers on the shoulder straps. (Brian L. Davis.)

forces gave up, he himself was considering withdrawing as his forces were virtually exhausted. Now, a greater success in France was assured.

On 22 June, France signed an armistice with Germany. For the first time Germany had taken on armies which were not only her equals, but were far superior in terms of numbers and theoretically capable of inflicting a terrible defeat on the *Wehrmacht*. However, the quality of leadership shown by the German generals surpassed that of their Allied counterparts. German generals such as Guderian and Rommel were enthusiastic exponents of the modern art of fast armoured warfare combined with powerful air support. Many Allied leaders still saw their strategy in outdated terms, more suited to the static battles of World War One.

With the Battle of France ended, Hitler turned his attention on Britain. Göring's *Luftwaffe* launched itself against the Royal Air Force's airfields in an attempt to subjugate Britain's air power and pave the way for the invasion of the UK: Operation SEALION. German air fleets from occupied Norway and France pounded their targets mercilessly, but the Royal Air Force was far from finished and by mid-November the *Luftwaffe* had shot its bolt. Göring then turned to night bombing, with massive raids being launched on London,

One of the top U-boat heroes of the war, Heinrich 'Ajax' Bleichrodt sank a total of 203,000 tons of enemy shipping. This represented 30 enemy ships and one destroyer. (Jak. P. Mallmann Showell/Dr Wolf Heinrich Bleichrodt.)

Vizeadmiral Bernhard Rogge, one of the few recipients of the rare Auxiliary Cruiser Badge with Diamonds, commanded the Auxiliary Cruiser **Atlantis**. After the war, he served with the West German navy, reaching the rank of Konteradmiral. (Jak P. Mallmann Showell.)

Oakleaves winner Heinrich 'Ajax' Bleichrodt posing with crew members of his boat, U-48. Bleichrodt won his Knight's Cross in 1940 in command of this boat with 7 U-Flotille. (Jak P. Mallmann Showell).

Coventry, Southampton and Birmingham which continued through the remainder of the year.

Throughout this period, Dönitz's U-boats had been taking a steady toll of Allied shipping, sinking over 1,000 ships representing over 400,000 tons, for the loss of 22 U-boats.

During 1940, in excess of 400 Knight's Crosses were awarded, plus seven Oakleaves to the Knight's Cross, introduced that year.

GROSSADMIRAL KARL DÖNITZ

Karl Dönitz was born on 16 September 1891 in Grünau, near Berlin, and joined the *Kaiserliche Marine* as an officer cadet in 1910. After six years service in surface vessels including the then ultra modern cruiser *Breslau*, Dönitz was posted as First Officer to *U-39*, and one year later was given command of his own boat, *UC-25*. By 1918, Dönitz was in command of the larger and more powerful *UC-68* when it was attacked and sunk by a British warship. Along with some of his crew, Dönitz was rescued and sent to a British Prisoner of War Camp. He was repatriated to Germany in 1919.

Dönitz remained in the navy after Germany's defeat but as his navy was no longer permitted a submarine force, he returned to surface duties, serving initially with a torpedo-boat unit. In 1928, he was appointed to command 4 Torpedoboots-Halbflotille before being posted to a staff position in Wilhelmshaven.

In November 1934, Dönitz, by now a Kapitän zur See, was given command of the cruiser *Emden* which he took on a goodwill cruise of the Indian Ocean. After this successful cruise, *Emden* was refitted and recommissioned with a new crew and a new Captain, Dönitz being posted back to the new U-boat arm of the navy to take command of U-Bootsflotille *Weddingen* in Kiel. This flotilla was named after one of Germany's great U-boat aces of World War One.

Dönitz saw the U-boat service expand from a small beginning to be one of the world's most powerful and deadly forces, and one which came perilously near to bringing Britain to its knees. Four weeks before the outbreak of war, Dönitz was appointed Befehlshaber der Unterseeboote (BdU). His enthusiasm for technical and tactical innovation, and his fatherly concern for his men were to be the hallmarks of Dönitz's 'reign' as BdU.

Hitler's knowledge of naval strategy was woefully inadequate and Germany's U-boat fleet still very weak, with only 39 seaworthy U-boats available at the start of hostilities. Dönitz's aggressive enthusiasm for U-boat warfare and his unhesitating support of his men soon led to the U-boat fleet scoring outstanding successes and growing greatly in Hitler's estimation. Günther Prien and his daring attack on Scapa Flow helped to convince Hitler of the need for the expansion of the U-boat arm. In recognition of his successful command of the U-boat fleet, Dönitz was awarded the Knight's Cross on 21 April 1940.

In January 1943, Admiral Dönitz was promoted to Commander-in-Chief of the navy with the rank of Grossadmiral, as successor to Grossadmiral Raeder.

This fine study shows Karl Dönitz as Befehlshaber der U-Boote. On the left breast of his jacket can be seen the U-boat Badge, the Bar to the Iron Cross, the Iron Cross First Class and, just visible, the U-Boat Badge of the Imperial German Navy (Jak P. Mallmann-Showell.)

This later photograph shows Dönitz after his promotion to Grossadmiral, wearing the massive gold braid sleeve rings of that rank and the Oakleaves to his Knight's Cross. (Chris Ailsby.)

This powerful position gave Dönitz considerable influence and this was used to continue his wholehearted support of the U-boat war. This support was reflected in the fact that by mid-1943, the *Kriegsmarine* had 212 operational U-boats, and a further 181 working up. On 6 April 1943, Grossadmiral Dönitz became the 223rd recipient of the Oakleaves, awarded in recognition of his command of the navy and of the U-boat arm in particular.

As Allied anti-submarine measures became more and more effective, and U-boats were destroyed faster than Germany's shipyards could build new ones and train new crews, Dönitz sought new and more advanced technology to redress the balance. Although German ship designers came up with the superb Type XXI U-boat, which if it had come into service earlier in the war, might well have turned the tables decisively, it was introduced too late to prevent inevitable German defeat. By 1945, thousands of trained sailors were being squandered as infantry in vain attempts to stem the Soviet tide on the Eastern Front.

Hitler had always been impressed by Dönitz and his strength of character and in April 1945 Dönitz was greatly surprised to learn that he had been appointed as Hitler's successor and that, Hitler having died, he was now Führer. This was a responsibility that Dönitz would have happily done without but his sense of duty dictated that he accept the burden of command of the shattered German Reich. One of his first moves was to abolish the title Führer and to regard himself simply as 'Head of State'.

It was during these last terrible days of the war that Dönitz achieved what he would consider to be his greatest triumph, the rescue of millions of refugees from the advancing Russians. Despite the desperate conditions, German seamen, both naval and merchant, willingly risked their lives time and time again bringing refugees through the perilous waters of the Baltic, under attack from Soviet aircraft and submarines.

Arrested with his staff on 23 May 1945 Dönitz was put on trial for war crimes at Nuremberg. Dönitz found considerable sympathy amongst many of his former enemies who accepted that his conduct of the U-boat war was no worse than the war conducted by their own submarine forces. Indeed, many US naval officers felt that the conduct of the war in the Pacific was far harsher and aggressive than the German conduct in the Atlantic.

Dönitz was cleared of 'crimes against humanity' but was found guilty on charges of 'waging aggressive war' and sentenced to ten years in prison. He served the full term. Despite his conviction, which many considered unfair, Dönitz retained the respect of many of his former enemies.

After his imprisonment ended, Dönitz retired to write his memoirs. A man of honour and one of history's great military leaders, Karl Dönitz died on 24 December 1980 at the age of 89. His coffin was carried to the grave by eight of his former U-boat Commanders, all bearers of the Knight's Cross.

KONTERADMIRAL ERICH BEY

Erich Bey was born in Hamburg in March 1898. His naval career started just after the outbreak of World War One and by the outbreak of World War Two, he was Flag Officer Destroyers, commanding 6 Destroyer Flotilla. Bey took part in the Battle of Narvik where the bulk of Germany's destroyer fleet was put out of action. During this battle, Bey was responsible for the destruction of two British warships, one through accurate gunfire and the other by ramming. For his part in the action, Bey was decorated with the Knight's Cross of the Iron Cross, only the seventh member of the *Kriegsmarine* to be so honoured, on 9 May 1940.

Bey, popularly known as 'Achmed' to his men, remained in the Norwegian theatre until December 1943 when, as commanding Konteradmiral, he was on the battlecruiser *Scharnhorst* during her attempt to intercept Convoy JW55B on its way to Russia. Unfortunately, the Royal Navy was aware of *Scharnhorst's* presence due to intercepted German signals. *Scharnhorst* lost her screen of escorting destroyers in bad weather and on the morning of 26 December, ran into the battleship HMS *Duke of York* with the cruiser HMS *Jamaica* from the south-west and the cruisers HMS *Belfast, Norfolk* and *Sheffield* from the north. *Scharnhorst* battled bravely against the odds until 17.45 hours when she sank in a freezing storm with the loss of all but 36 of her crew. Konteradmiral Erich Bey was amongst those lost.

The British sailors on the opposing ships were much impressed by the gallantry of *Scharnhorst's* crew and dropped a wreath over her last position, a fitting tribute to Bey and all his gallant sailors.

Kapitän zur See Erich 'Achmed' Bey. On the lapel is worn the 1939 Bar to the Iron Cross Second Class of 1914 and just visible below the Iron Cross First Class on the left breast is the Destroyer War Badge. (F. J. Stephens.)

Generalmajor Bruno Bräuer. This illustration is one of a series of postcards by the famous war artist Wolfgang Willrich. It shows Bräuer wearing the parachutists smock and the famous rimless German parachutists helmet. (Author Collection.)

GENERALMAJOR BRUNO BRÄUER

Born in Berlin in February 1893, Bruno Bräuer was a veteran of World War One where he had served as an Army NCO, winning the Iron Cross Second Class. After the war, Bräuer joined the Prussian security police and, following the Nazi rise to power in 1933, served as a Company Commander in Polizeiabteilung Wecke, a 400-strong unit of politically reliable men commanded by Polizeimajor Wecke. This group evolved into Landespolizeigruppe General Göring, Göring being Prussian Minister of the Interior at this time, and further into Regiment *General Göring*. When Hitler introduced conscription in 1935, Göring gave this order:

The Regiment *General Göring* will be transferred into the *Luftwaffe* on 1 October 1935. From the volunteers of the regiment, a paratroop batallion is to be formed as a cadre for the future German Paratroop force.

Bruno Bräuer was one of these very first volunteers, taking part in the first training course at the Paratroop Training School at Stendal. He was the first Commander of 1 Kompanie/Fallschirmjäger Regiment 1 and by 1938, was Commander of the entire regiment, holding the rank of Oberst.

Bräuer saw action with Fallschirmjäger Regiment 1 when it was used in the attack on Holland. Bräuer personally led his men into action during the capture of the Moerdyk and Dodrecht Bridges. For his personal daring and his command of the regiment, he was decorated with the Knight's Cross on 24 May 1940.

The classic battle fought by the German Fallschirmtruppe was, of course, the airborne invasion of Crete. During this battle, Bräuer once again led his regiment into action at Heraklion where it suffered heavy casualties until relieved by the Army's 5 Gebirgsdivision. Although the invasion of Crete was a success, the losses sustained were horrendous and Hitler was loath to commit his Fallschirmjäger in the airborne role again.

The Fallschirmjäger next saw action on the Eastern Front where they were used in an infantry role. Fallschirmjäger Regiment 1 under the command of Oberst Bräuer was located on the Leningrad front on the south bank of the River Newa and acquitted itself well in the furious battles around the bridgehead the Soviets had established on the river, and the Soviets were eventually thrown back. The first winter of the Eastern Campaign had cost the *Luftwaffe* the lives of 3000 Fallschirmjäger, many of whom were veterans who had fought in Belgium, Holland and Crete.

After his period of service on the Eastern Front, Bräuer returned to Crete as the Commander of the occupation garrison. Although the relationship between the German occupation troops and the native Cretans was initially quite good, German ruthless suppression of partisan activity soon led to a deterioration. Bräuer eventually fell out of favour with his own high command and was finally placed on the reserve list.

Recalled to active service in December 1944, Bräuer, by then holding the rank of Generalmajor, was given command of 9 Fallschirmdivision which was stationed partly at Berlin and partly at Breslau. The Division was decimated during the final battles of the war and surrendered to the Soviets in May 1945.

Bräuer was handed over to the Greek authorities who tried and executed him for alleged excesses against partisans on Crete. Whatever the validity or otherwise of these charges, there is no refuting Bräuer's personal bravery and the high regard in which he was held by his Fallschirmjäger.

GENERALFELDMARSCHALL ERNST BUSCH

Ernst Busch was born on 6 July 1885 in Essen-Steele, Westphalia. He embarked on his long and successful military career as an army officer in June 1904 when he was commissioned as an infantry Leutnant at the age of just 19 years. When war broke out in 1914, Busch was serving as an Oberleutnant in an infantry regiment. Two years later, whilst serving in France as a Hauptmann, Busch was decorated with the covetted 'Blue Max', or *Pour le Mérite*, for his distinguished service.

Busch remained with Germany's tiny post-war army and his career continued to progress satisfactorily. So much so that when Hitler came to power in 1933, Busch had also reached the rank of full colonel and was a Regimental

Commander. His next promotion, to the rank of Generalmajor, came in 1935 when he was given command of 23 Infanterie Division. On the outbreak of war in 1939, Busch had reached the rank of General der Infanterie and commanded VIII Armee Korps.

Shortly after the invasion of Poland, Busch was given command of XVI Armee Korps which he led during the campaign in the West. Busch's forces were part of Armeegruppe 'A' which attacked through Luxembourg into France against the French 2 and 3 Armies commanded by Huntziger and Conde. For his successful leadership during this campaign, Busch was awarded the Knight's Cross on 26 May 1940 and promoted to Generaloberst.

Busch continued his command of XVI Armee on the Northern Sector of the Eastern Front following the invasion of the Soviet Union. For his skill in command of this same army, Busch was promoted to Generalfeldmarschall in February 1943 and in August of that year became the 274th recipient of the Oakleaves. Generalfeldmarschall Busch was subsequently given command of Heeresgruppe 'Mitte' which was decimated around Minsk later in 1943 and eventually retreated into Poland.

Busch was moved to the Western Front in March 1945 and became Oberbefehlshaber Nordwest, operating around Flensburg. He was taken prisoner by the British when Germany surrendered. Busch died in British captivity in Aldershot in July 1945.

In this portrait study, Generalfeldmarschall Ernst Busch wears the **Pour le Mérite** *just below the Knight's Cross with Oakleaves. (Author Collection.)*

Adolf Galland, one of Germany's top fighter aces. On his right sleeve is the cuff title of his unit, Jagdgeschwader 'Schlageter'. The rare Pilot/ Observer Badge with Diamonds is being worn on the left breast pocket.

GENERALLEUTNANT ADOLF GALLAND

Adolf Galland was born in Westerhalt in March 1912 and was to become one of the *Luftwaffe*'s most famous and successful fighter pilots. His military career began in 1934 when he joined Infanterie Regiment 10 in Dresden for basic military training. He was commissioned as a Leutnant in October 1934. The German armed forces at this time were not permitted an air force but when all attempts to conceal Göring's fledgling *Luftwaffe* were abandoned in 1935, Galland officially became a member of Jagdgeschwader 2 *Richthofen*. During the Spanish Civil War, Galland gained invaluable combat experience with the *Legion Condor*. He became one of only 27 Spanish Cross with Diamonds recipients.

During the Polish Campaign, Oberleutnant Galland flew the obsolescent Henschel HS 126 biplane fighter. He won the Iron Cross Second Class and was promoted to Hauptmann in October of 1939. The Western Campaign found Galland with Jagdgeschwader 27, flying the fast, modern Messerschmitt Bf109 fighter. Later, he became commander of III/Jagdgeschwader 26. Between 12 May and 9 June 1940, he shot down twelve enemy aircraft. On 1 August 1940, Galland, now a Major, was awarded the Knight's Cross after gaining his seventeenth victory. He became Kommodore of Jagdgeschwader 26 on 22 August and led this elite unit during the Battle of Britain. By 25 September, Major Galland's score had reached 40, bringing him the Oakleaves to his Knight's Cross. He was summoned to the Reichskanzlei in Berlin where Hitler presented the Oakleaves to him personally. On 1 November, he was promoted to the rank of Oberstleutnant.

On 21 June 1941, still on the Western Front, Oberstleutnant Galland was awarded the Swords in recognition of having reached his 69th victory. On 9 August 1941, Galland discovered that one of the English fighter pilots shot down by his squadron that day was none other than Douglas Bader. A sporting and gallant opponent, Galland had Bader invited to his airfield where he was allowed to sit at the controls of his Bf109, before being sent on his way with a box of Galland's best cigars. After the war, Galland and Bader were to become good friends.

On 4 December 1941, Galland was promoted to Oberst and on 28 January 1942, he was presented with the Diamonds after his victory score reached 94. It is interesting to note that Göring, on seeing Galland's Diamonds, became very annoyed, saying that the stones were not real. Göring raised the matter with Hitler saying that Germany's highest award should not be presented with fake stones. Göring then arranged for a set with perfect stones to be provided. Hitler, unaware of this, had done the same. Galland, therefore, had three sets of Diamonds presented to him. Then, when his Diamonds were lost in an air raid on his home town, Göring had yet another set made for him!

Following the death of Galland's good friend and comrade Werner Mölders in an aircraft crash, Galland was nominated as Mölders' successor as Inspector General of Fighters. In November 1942, Galland was promoted to the rank of Generalmajor, thus becoming the youngest General in the German armed forces, at the age of just 30.

On 22 May 1943, Galland witnessed the test flight of the new Messerschmitt Me 262 jet and was greatly impressed. Having tried out the new aircraft himself, Galland felt that even at this stage of the war, Germany could regain air superiority if the new fighter were put into production. In his position as General of Fighters, Galland was keen to apply new technology. Hitler, however, insisted that the new jet aircraft be used as a bomber. This was but one of many occasions on which he was to find himself at loggerheads with high command. Galland was nobody's 'yes-man'. His tendency was to take the part of the fighting man at the front against the bureaucracy higher leadership. He eventually fell from favour and was relieved of his position in January 1945.

Galland's last post was with Jagdverband 44, flying the superb Me 262, as a fighter. This was the so-called 'Squadron of Experts' in which almost every pilot was an experienced fighter ace bearing the Knight's Cross.

Galland ended the war as he had begun, as a front line fighter pilot. His final rank was Generalleutnant. He had flown over 400 missions flown during the war, plus nearly 300 in Spain, and had a total of 104 victories. Whilst Galland's victory score is much lower than some of Germany's great aces, it must be remembered that they were scored against skilled British and American pilots, and that for a considerable period of the war, Galland was in a staff position, where he was not flying combat missions. When looked at in this light, Adolf Galland's score places him as one of the greatest fighter aces of the war.

Galland ended the war with the respect of friend and foe alike. He had used his position as General of Fighters to help and support the front line fighter pilot as much as possible. Indeed, when Göring cast a slur on the bravery and fighting ability of his fighter pilots, Galland removed all his decorations and refused to wear them in protest at this slur.

After the war, Adolf Galland went on to become a successful businessman. His excellent book, *The First and The Last*, detailing the history of the German fighter arm has been translated into fifteen languages and has sold over three million copies. Galland's standing amongst his former enemies is well illustrated by the number of invitations he has received to attend reunions of Allied wartime pilots. As a guest at the opening of the RAF Museum at Hendon, he spent a considerable time conversing with the heir to the British throne, Prince Charles, along with his close friend, British ace Bob Stanford-Tuck. Adolf Galland now lives in retirement at his home near Bonn.

OBERST WALTER OESAU

Walter 'Gulle' Oesau was born in 1913 in Farnewinkel, the son of a bank director. After completing his term of service in the Reichsarbeitsdienst he entered military service with 2 Artillerie Regiment in Itzehoe, but his ambition had always been to fly. After attending flight training school and the Hannover War School, he qualified as a pilot and was posted to Jagdgeschwader *Richthofen*. Oesau served in the *Legion Condor* during the Spanish Civil War and was one of only 27 recipients of the Spanish Cross with Diamonds. During his time in Spain, he gained eight victories.

His first combat assignment in World War Two was in the Western Campaign and by mid-August 1940 had scored 20 victories, winning the Knight's Cross for this achievement. Oesau had won the Iron Cross Second Class for his fourth victory and was the first pilot in his group to win the Iron Cross First Class. By February 1941, Oesau's score had risen to 40, winning him the Oakleaves to his Knight's Cross. He was only the ninth recipient of this coveted decoration and only the fourth recipient in the *Luftwaffe*.

Oesau's squadron was posted to the Eastern Front in June 1941 and as the German onslaught fell upon the woefully unprepared Soviets, Oesau rapidly increased his score, shooting down sixteen Soviet aircraft in sixteen days. In a single engagement Oesau and one other pilot from the squadron shot down seven enemy planes in 20 minutes. By 15 July 1941, his score had reached 78 and he became only the third recipient of the recently instituted Swords, which were personally presented to him by Adolf Hitler.

Shortly afterwards, Oesau, by now holding the rank of Major, was posted back to the Western Front and before long, his one hundredth victim, a Spitfire, had fallen.

On reaching this score, Oesau was forbidden to fly any further combat missions, such experienced 'aces' as he being too valuable to risk losing. However, the necessities of war meant that Oesau was taking to the air again before too much longer and his score continued to grow. By May 1944, he had taken his score to 125. Shortly before the Allied invasion of Normandy, Oesau was flying a combat mission over the Eiffel mountains when he was bounced by a United States Army Air Force's P-38 Lightning fighter and shot down. Oesau had died a hero's death, a true 'ace' and a gallant airman.

On his flying jacket, Oberst Walter Oesau wears the Spanish Cross with Diamonds on the right breast and the Iron Cross First Class and Spanish Wound Badge on the left breast. At the neck, he wears his Knight's Cross with Swords and Oakleaves. (Author Collection.)

At the time of this photograph, Oberst Herbert Ihlefeld held the rank of Oberstleutnant as shown from the rank insignia on his tunic. (Herbert Ihlefeld.)

SS-BRIGADEFÜHRER UND GENERALMAJOR DER WAFFEN-SS FRITZ WITT

One of the original members of the elite *Leibstandarte*, Fritz Witt had been born in Hohenlimburg in May 1908. During the Polish Campaign, Witt served as an SS-Hauptsturmführer and Company Commander, earning both the Second and First Class Iron Crosses. Given command of 1 Bat./SS-Standarte *Deutschland* in October 1939, he led this unit during the campaign in the West with great success. On 27 May 1940, Witt's troops successfully repulsed a strong British attack with armoured support and held the battalion's position, destroying nine of the enemy tanks in the process. During the latter part of the campaign, the regiment took part in heavy hand to hand fighting around Langnes where over 20,000 prisoners were taken. For his part in the successful Western campaign, Fritz Witt was awarded the Knight's Cross on 4 September 1940. Shortly afterwards, he was transferred back to the *Leibstandarte*.

During the Balkan Campaign, Witt further established himself as a daring and resourceful officer, several times personally leading his men in fierce hand to hand combat. When the attack on Rostov was launched in the winter of 1941, the *Leibstandarte* was in the forefront of the fighting and once again Witt distinguished himself in these battles. He was awarded the German Cross in Gold in June 1942, at which time he commanded SS-Panzer Grenadier Regiment 1.

After refitting in France during the second half of 1942, the *Leibstandarte* returned to the Eastern Front, upgraded as a Panzer Grenadier Division. Scarcely had it returned when it was thrown into the thick of the fighting in

45

the Donez basin. Two battalions of SS Panzer Grenadier Regiment 1 held a sector of the front over 32 kilometres long. Soviet attacking units were heavily mauled by the defending SS Grenadiers. For his command of the regiment during this period, Witt, by now an SS-Standartenführer, became the 200th recipient of the Oakleaves on 1 March 1943.

Shortly afterwards, Witt was given command of the newly formed 12 SS Panzer Division *Hitlerjugend*. This division was formed from a combination of young grenadiers from the Hitler Youth and a cadre of experienced veterans from the *Leibstandarte*, as well as a few from the army. Witt was exactly the type of Divisional Commander that these young men could relate to and his bold and daring style of leadership ensured his immense popularity.

Hitlerjugend was the first Waffen-SS unit to be committed to battle in Normandy and proved itself a deadly opponent to the British and Canadian forces which opposed it. Only a few days after the invasion, Witt was relaxing at his command post during a lull in the fighting when a barrage from Allied ships offshore landed right on top of the position. Witt was killed before he could reach the safety of a trench. The death of this popular officer was a sad loss to the Division and to all his comrades of the *Leibstandarte*. Fritz Witt is buried at the German War Cemetery at La Cambe.

OBERST HERBERT IHLEFELD

Born in June 1914 in Pinnow, Pomerania, Herbert Ihlefeld flew with the *Legion Condor* in Spain during the Civil War. He served alongside other top pilots such as Adolf Galland, Werner Mölders and Walter Oesau. His time in Spain was a successful one and by the start of World War Two, he was already an experienced ace with seven victories to his credit.

During the attack in the West, Ihlefeld flew with 1 Lehrgeschwader 2, which he also eventually commanded from late summer 1940 until spring 1942. He was decorated with the Knight's Cross on 13 September 1940 on achieving his 21st victory during the Battle of Britain.

On 27 June 1941, Ihlefeld was awarded the Oakleaves in recognition of his 40th victory, and on 22 April 1942, he became the fifth fighter pilot to reach the score of 100 victories. The award of the coveted Swords followed just two days later, by which time he had added a further 'kill' to his score.

Herbert Ihlefeld went on to command some of the *Luftwaffe*'s finest fighter units, including Jagdgeschwader 52 and Jagdgeschwader 1. By the end of the war, Ihlefeld had flown over one thousand sorties and had a final score of over 130 victories. Oberst Ihlefeld survived the war and now lives in retirement.

MAJOR HELMUT WICK

One of the *Luftwaffe*'s top Battle of Britain aces, Helmut Wick was born in August 1915 in Mannheim, the son of a forester. Somewhat of a tearaway, Wick was always in trouble for playing truant and it was all his father could do to make him finish his schooling. This rebellious attitude to authority was to mark his military career, too. However, thanks to his father's influence, Wick did finish his studies and eventually joined the fledgling *Luftwaffe* in 1936.

Wick scored his first victory in November 1939 whilst flying as a Leutnant with 1 Jagdgeschwader 53 in France. This was to be the start of a meteoric career for the young flyer. Within only eight months he had increased his score to 20 and was awarded the Knight's Cross on 27 August 1940. At this point in the war, 20, in general terms, was the normal required score for the award of the Knight's Cross to a fighter pilot (some aces, for no specific reasons, were kept waiting much longer). From then on, Wick's scoring rate really took off and within only six weeks he had doubled his score. This brought Wick the Oakleaves to his Knight's Cross, the award being made on 6 October.

On 28 November 1940, Wick's luck ran out. Engaged by Flying Officer John Dundas in combat over the Isle of Wight, his Bf109 was seriously damaged. Wick baled out and was seen to land in the water, but he was never found.

Wick was a tremendously popular officer, his total disregard for authority making him particularly well liked by his younger comrades. To them, he had become something of a hero. At the time of his death, Wick held the rank of Major and was Kommodore of JG2 *Richthofen*, with 56 victories to his credit. Wick's achievements were particularly impressive in view of the very short period over which they were scored.

KAPITÄN ZUR SEE FRIEDRICH BONTE

Born in 1896, Friedrich Bonte was the commander of 2 Zerstörer Flotille on the outbreak of war but handed over this command to Korvettenkapitän von Pufendorf in October 1939. Bonte himself was made Führer der Zerstörer in November, thus commanding all Destroyer Flotillas. As Commodore of Destroyers, Bonte was responsible directly to the Fleet Commander.

Major Helmut Wick, one of the Luftwaffe's most charismatic Battle of Britain personalities.

Friedrich Bonte, Kommodore of Destroyers. (F. J. Stephens.)

During April 1940, Bonte commanded Kampfgruppe Narvik during the invasion of Norway and was an important contributor to the success of the invasion, codenamed unternehmung WESERÜBUNG NORD. His flag flew from the Destroyer *Z-21 Wilhelm Heidkamp*, a 2,400-tonner of the 'Von Roeder' class, armed with five 5-inch guns.

At 4.30am on the morning of 10 April 1940, the British warships *Hardy*, *Hunter* and *Havock*, all 'H' class destroyers, carried out a surprise attack on the German force, firing off five torpedoes each and also opening fire with their main armament. The Germans were caught totally unawares and *Z-21* was hit by the first torpedo. This caused an enormous explosion, killing Bonte and so seriously damaging the ship that it capsized the next day.

In recognition of the important part which he had played with his Kampf-gruppe Narvik in the success of the invasion, Bonte was posthumously awarded the Knight's Cross on 17 October 1940.

KORVETTENKAPITÄN WOLFGANG LÜTH

Born in Riga in October 1913, Wolfgang Lüth was to become one of history's most successful submarine commanders. He was commissioned Leutnant zur See on 1 October 1936 and two years later, promoted to Oberleutnant, entered the U-boat service. Lüth was given his first command, *U-9*, in January 1940 and in only five operations sank over 16,000 tons of enemy shipping. Following this, he was given command of *U-138*, a Type IID submarine of 1 U-Bootsflotille. He increased his score to 49,000 tons after only two operations with this boat. For this achievement, he was decorated with the Knight's Cross on 24 October 1940. Lüth subsequently commanded *U-43* from November

Korvettenkapitän Wolfgang Lüth with his friend and fellow U-boat ace Erich Topp. Lüth is wearing a leather double breasted 'Reefer' jacket of the type often used by U-boat personnel. (Jak P. Mallmann Showell.)

Lüth, at a social function with his crew members. The Spanish Cross can just be discerned on the right breast of Lüth's jacket.

Judging from Lüth's expression, the Matrosenobergefreiter at his side must have told a very funny joke! (Otto Giese.)

1940 for the next sixteen months, at the end of which he had sunk 81,950 tons of enemy shipping.

In May 1942, he was given a new vessel, *U-181*. This was a Type IXD-2, a more powerful craft with a greater radius of action than previous U-boats. He was tasked with taking her into the Indian Ocean and striking at Allied merchant vessels there. This cruise was to last an amazing 203 days. It was to the great credit of Lüth and his men that they carried out this cruise with great success. *U-181* set a new endurance record with this spell of over six months at sea. In recognition of *U-181*'s achievement, Lüth received the Oakleaves to his Knight's Cross in November 1942.

Lüth's next cruise was also a long one, lasting 130 days. Within just two cruises, Lüth had clocked up nearly a whole year at sea and had increased his score to 103,712 tons. On 15 April 1943, Lüth received the Swords and with his success continuing unabated, the Diamonds followed in August of the same year.

By this time, Lüth had sunk over 253,000 tons of enemy shipping. Appreciating the value of Lüth's experience, Dönitz had him transferred to a shore position, as an instructor at the Murwik Naval School. His great expertise was to be put to good use in training new sailors for the U-boat arm.

During the closing days of the war, Lüth found himself attached to Dönitz's headquarters. After the capitulation, many foreign labourers who had been forcibly brought to Germany roamed free looting and pillaging. The Allied occupation authorities appreciated the danger this posed and allowed German sentries to retain their small arms for defence. One evening when approaching a sentry post, Lüth was challenged by the German sentry. He did not hear the sentry's challenge and the sentry opened fire, killing him instantly. This must be one of the war's most ironic deaths, for a U-boat man to survive years of danger, only to be killed by one of his own sentries after the war had ended.

1941
THE YEAR OF VICTORIES

The start of 1941 saw the continuance of the air war with both the *Luftwaffe* and the Royal Air Force making heavy raids on each other's cities. The war at sea saw some minor successes for the *Kriegsmarine* in January when the auxiliary cruiser *Pinguin* captured an entire Norwegian whaling fleet, and in February when the heavy cruiser *Admiral Hipper* sank seven ships from an Allied convoy. The battlecruisers *Gneisenau* and *Scharnhorst* also scored some successes in anti-shipping sorties.

Rommel's Afrika Korps arrived in North Africa in February and was soon in action against the British who quickly realised that they were up against a totally different class of opposition to the Italian troops they had been fighting previously.

In March came tragedy for the *Kriegsmarine*. Within the one month, its top three U-boat aces, Günther Prien, Otto Kretschmer and Joachim Shepke, were lost. Luckily for Kretschmer, he survived the sinking of his U-boat and spent the rest of the war as a prisoner.

On land, however, things were going much better and Rommel opened his first offensive against the British, quickly capturing El Agheila. The German invasion of Greece and Jugoslavia began on Sunday, 6 April. The opposition in Jugoslavia was quickly crushed, an armistice being signed only eleven days later. All the while, Rommel's troops continued to advance, capturing Bardia, Sollum and the vital Halfaya Pass, or 'Hellfire Pass' as it was commonly known to the British troops.

The airborne invasion of Crete began on 20 May and by the end of the month, the Germans had defeated the Allied defenders but at such a cost to themselves that Hitler would never approve of another airborne operation for his Fallschirmjäger. For the *Kriegsmarine*, May was a month for great victory and tragic defeat. Victory when the pride of the British Navy, HMS *Hood* was sunk by the *Bismarck*, and tragedy when the *Bismarck* herself was sent to the bottom of the sea only three days later.

All other German operations so far, however, were to pale into insignificance by comparison when Hitler launched Operation BARBAROSSA, the invasion of the Soviet Union, on 22 June. Initial German successes were phenomenal as the *Luftwaffe* smashed the bulk of the Red Air Force's combat units on the ground and the land forces thrust forward sweeping away all opposition. The German armies were advancing as fast as the Soviets could retreat. During this period, many Russians welcomed the Germans as liberators. This state of affairs was to be short lived, however, as second echelon security troops moved in and partisan activity increased.

In the meantime, German advances progressed well and in mid-July the German armies cut off and captured over 300,000 Red Army troops at the battle of Smolensk and by early August a total of 895,000 enemy prisoners had

U-boat ace Erich Topp, second from right, with two of his peers, Heinrich Bleichrodt and Wolfgang Lüth. Topp joined the ranks of the Knight's Cross winners in June 1941. (Jak P. Mallmann Showell.)

Dr Heinrich Neumann, Medical Officer with the Fallschirmjäger Sturmregiment. Neumann was decorated with the Knight's Cross on 21 August 1941 for actions on the Eastern Front. Of particular interest in this photograph is the cloth embroidered Iron Cross First Class. A real rarity! (Josef Charita.)

General Hasso von Manteuffel shakes hands with Hitler. General von Manteuffel commanded the elite **Grossdeustchland** Division and wears the divisional sleeveband on his right cuff above the Africa Campaign cuff title, and wears the rare Panzer Assault Badge for 25 engagements with the enemy. (Richard Schulze-Kossens)

been taken within a space of only six weeks since the beginning of the campaign. During the following month a further 600,000 prisoners were taken during battles around Kiev. Also during September, Operation TYPHOON, the drive on Moscow was launched.

In October, Kharkov was captured and in November, Kursk and Rostov. By the end of November, the Germans were only 30 kilometres from Moscow. Ultimately, the advance stalled with leading German units already in the Moscow suburbs, and only 19 kilometres from the city centre. On 5 December, the Soviets launched a major counter-attack and the Germans, so near to their goal, were forced to retreat. Woefully unprepared for the horrors of a Russian winter, the average German soldier suffered terribly and gradually the Soviet counter-attacks began to tell.

On 11 December, Germany declared war on the United States of America and this gave the *Kriegsmarine*'s U-boat commanders a golden opportunity for targets on the lucrative American coastline. During 1941, Allied shipping losses totalled 4,389,000 tons. This figure represented over 1,200 ships.

All in all, the year had been a great success for Germany's armed forces, although by the year's end it had become apparent that Hitler's plans for a rapid subjugation of Russia were totally unrealistic. With so many campaigns being conducted during the year, and the number of soldiers seeing combat increasing dramatically, the number of awards of the Knight's Cross also increased. A total of around 786 Knight's Crosses were awarded, 50 Oakleaves and five Swords, four of which were awarded to *Luftwaffe* fighter aces.

FREGATTENKAPITÄN HEINRICH LEHMANN-WILLENBROCK

Born in Bremen in December 1911, Heinrich Lehmann-Willenbrock joined the *Reichsmarine* in 1931 at the age of 20. Initially serving with the surface fleet, he volunteered for the U-boat service in 1939 and in September 1940 was given his first command, the Type VIIC vessel *U-96*, serving with 7 Unterseebootsflotille.

Kapitänleutnant Lehmann-Willenbrock carried out eight war cruises between April 1940 and March 1942, all with *U-96*. On 26 February 1941, he was decorated with the Knight's Cross after achieving a score of sixteen enemy ships sunk within a period of only three months. By 31 December of that year he had added the Oakleaves to his Knight's Cross, the 51st recipient of this covetted award. In May 1942, he was appointed to command 9 U-Flotille at Brest and in December 1944 he took command of 11 U-Flotille at Narvik.

Lehmann-Willenbrock was the eighth most successful of all the U-boat aces, having sunk 28 enemy ships, totalling 205,000 tons. He survived the war and went on to a successful career in the West German merchant navy.

Lehmann-Willenbrock's submarine, *U-96*, was to become the subject of the best selling novel and subsequent widely acclaimed film *Das Boot*. The author of

Fregattenkapitän Heinrich Lehmann-Willenbrock with the mascot of the 9 U-Flotille. Like the Flotilla's U-boats, the goat also wears the Flotilla crest of the sawfish. The wearing of jackboots is unusual amongst naval officers who usually wore long trousers and shoes. (Jak P. Mallmann Showell.)

As Flotilla Commander, Lehmann-Willenbrock *from sea, Kluth is unshaven and wears U-boat*
greets one of his returning U-boat Captains, *overalls. (Jak P. Mallmann Showell.)*
Gerhard Kluth of U-377. Having just returned

the novel, Lothar-Günther Buchheim, was a Naval War Correspondent during the war and had served with Lehmann-Willenbrock aboard *U-96*. The real life *U-96* survived the horrors of the U-boat war in the Atlantic only to be sunk by Allied bombers whilst tied up, unmanned at Wilhelmshaven.

SS-STANDARTENFÜHRER FRITZ KLINGENBERG

Fritz Klingenberg was born on 17 December 1912, the son of a dairyman from Röwershagen. He joined the SS-Verfügungstruppe in 1934 and was amongst the first intake to the SS Junkerschule at Bad Tölz in Bavaria. Promoted to SS-Untersturmführer on commissioning, he was posted as a Platoon Commander in the *Germania* Standarte before being assigned to the staff of the Inspectorate of the SS-Verfügungstruppe. During the French Campaign, he served as the Divisional Adjutant to the SS-Verfügungsdivision, winning both the Second and First Class Iron Crosses.

The opening of the Balkan Campaign saw Klingenberg with the rank of SS-Hauptsturmführer commanding the Kradschützenkompanie of the SS *Reich* Division (later to become the *Das Reich* SS Panzer Division). The *Reich* Division together with the army's elite *Grossdeutschland* Division were moving towards Belgrade during the invasion of Jugoslavia. Klingenberg's motorcycle recce company reached the banks of the Danube. In typical daredevil fashion, Klingenberg commandeered a launch and with only eleven other men, set off into the Jugoslav capital. As luck would have it, he bumped into the German Military Attaché, Oberst Toussaint. Sizing up the situation, Klingenberg and Toussaint located the Mayor of Belgrade and persuaded him that it would be in the best interests of his people to surrender the city peacefully and avoid bloodshed. At the time Klingenberg entered the city there were no other German troops in Belgrade. His daring exploit allowed the capture of the city without losses and was a great propaganda coup for Germany. At the conclusion of the campaign, Klingenberg was personally received by Hitler and decorated with the Knight's Cross on 14 May 1941.

Klingenberg's subsequent assignments included service at Bad Tölz where he was involved in the training of officer candidates from the foreign volunteer units of the Waffen-SS. His last assignment was as the commander of 17 SS Panzer Grenadier Division *Götz von Berlichingen* with the rank of SS-Standartenführer, in January 1945. During a particularly fierce battle with US armoured forces near Herxheim, he fell in battle on 22 March 1945.

LEUTNANT DER RESERVE ARTUR BECKER-NEETZ

Artur Becker-Neetz was born in Danzig on 31 December 1920, the son of architect Georg Becker. He attended the Realgymnasium of St Johann in Danzig, obtaining his leaving certificate on 8 March 1938. From April 1938 to March 1939, he served with the Danzig State Labour Service before commencing studies in construction engineering at the Technical High School in Danzig.

On 3 July 1939, he enlisted as a volunteer in Infanterie Regiment 243 in Danzig, and from 1 September 1939, saw action in the Polish Campaign around Gotenhafen and Modlin. During the French Campaign, he was awarded the Iron Cross Second Class on 24 June 1940 and, on 1 July, was promoted to Unteroffizier. On 6 July, he qualified for the Infantry Assault Badge.

By the opening of Operation BARBAROSSA on 22 June 1941, he was serving with 7 Kompanie of Fusilier Regiment 394 and was decorated with the Iron Cross First Class on 26 July 1941. During an operation to secure the flanks of the Regiment in the area to the south of Mogilev, east of the Dnieper, Unteroffizier Becker-Neetz took control after all of the officers present had been killed or wounded. Rallying his men with shouts and cheers, he continued to lead them against the enemy even after suffering a severe head-wound from a shot which passed straight through his steel helmet. For this and subsequent meritorious actions, he was awarded the Knight's Cross on 25 August 1941.

After hospital treatment in Frankfurt and long convalescent leave, he attended Officer Candidate Training in Wischau, near Brünn, and was commissioned as Leutnant der Reserve on 1 December 1943. From then on until the end of the war he was an instructor at a sniper course in Denmark.

At the end of the war Leutnant Becker-Neetz was taken prisoner by the British and held in captivity until September 1945. After his release, he returned to his studies as a construction engineer, graduating in 1949. Today, Artur Becker-Neetz is an official of the Ordensgemeinschaft der Ritterkreuzträger.

At the time of this photograph,
Standartenführer Fritz Klingenberg was a
Hauptsturmführer with 2/Kradsschützen
Bataillon Das Reich. His Knight's Cross was
awarded on 14 May 1941. (Arthur Charlton.)

At the time of the award of his Oakleaves,
Korvettenkapitän Adalbert Schnee held the rank
of Kapitänleutnant and was in command of
U-201. (Adalbert Schnee.)

Artur Becker-Neetz as an Unteroffizier with 7
Kompanie, Schützen Regiment 394,
photographed in April 1943. (Artur Becker-
Neetz.)

A later photograph, taken in January 1945,
after Becker-Neetz had been commissioned as a
Leutnant. (Artur Becker-Neetz.)

KORVETTENKAPITÄN ADALBERT SCHNEE

One of Germany's most popular U-boat commanders, Adalbert Schnee was born in Berlin in 1913. He was to become known as somewhat of an expert in destroying convoy escorts and amongst a total score of 27 ships destroyed, representing some 190,000 tons, were included an auxiliary cruiser, a destroyer and a submarine-chaser. Schnee was decorated with the Knight's Cross on 30 August 1941 as Kapitänleutnant in command of *U-201*, the Oakleaves following on 15 July 1942. However, in view of his experiences against escort vessels, Schnee was ultimately taken off sea duties and appointed to a post with the Oberkommando der *Wehrmacht* in 1944. He was an acknowledged 'expert' on convoy attacks.

Towards the end of the war, Schnee was given command of one of the ultra modern Type XXI 'Electro' boats, *U-2511*, serving with the 31 U-Flotille. These Type XXI boats may well have altered the course of the war, and history, had the *Kriegsmarine* had them in sufficient numbers in time. However, no matter how advanced they were, they entered service too late to have any effect on the final outcome of the war.

Schnee took *U-2511* on its first operational war cruise in May 1945. Awaiting a convoy target, he received a signal warning him that in view of the imminent ending of hostilities, no Allied ships should be attacked. On his return journey to port, however, he did try some dummy runs against Allied shipping and found that he could quite easily have attacked, undetected, and sunk the British cruiser HMS *Norfolk*. Remembering his order, however, he allowed her to pass unmolested.

Schnee survived the war and became a noted member of the Verband deutscher U-Bootfahrer. He died in 1982.

SS-BRIGADEFÜHRER THEODOR WISCH

Theodor Wisch was born on 13 December 1907 at Wesselburener Koog in Schleswig-Holstein, the son of a farmer. After completing a diploma course in agriculture, he became one of the first volunteers accepted by the elite *Leibstandarte* in the spring of 1933. He was commissioned as an SS-Untersturmführer later that same year.

Wisch served in the Polish Campaign as a Company Commander, winning the Iron Cross Second Class in September 1939 and the First Class in November. By the opening of the Western Campaign, Wisch was serving as a Battalion Commander and saw action in the Balkan Campaign in the same capacity.

In the autumn of 1941, Wisch, at this point holding the rank of SS-Sturmbannführer, was in command of II Bat./LSSAH on the Eastern Front. Wisch and his unit were instrumental in an attack to free an encircled German unit. Despite the overwhelming odds against him Wisch succeeded in his task, threw back the enemy and freed his encircled comrades. For this achievement, he received the Knight's Cross on 15 September 1941.

During the Battle of Kharkov in February 1943, Wisch was awarded the German Cross in Gold.

After a brief spell of duty in Italy, the *Leibstandarte* returned to the Eastern Front, refitted as a Panzer Division. It was thrown into the fighting at Tarnopol and the Dnieper battles. Encircled along with 1 Panzer Armee at Kamenez, the division only broke out of the encirclement with heavy losses. On 12 February 1944, Wisch was awarded the Oakleaves for his command of the division during this period.

After the breakout, the division was withdrawn from the front and sent to Belgium for rest and refitting. With the Allied invasion of Normandy in June 1944, it was thrown into battle on 18 June and fought alongside the 12 SS Panzer Division *Hitlerjugend* in the furious combat around Caen and later through the Falaise Gap. On 28 August 1944, Wisch, by now an SS-Brigadeführer, was awarded the Swords in recognition of his command of the division during the Normandy battles.

Wisch survived the war, holding the rank of Brigadeführer and General-major der Waffen-SS. He now lives in retirement in Schleswig-Holstein.

OBERSTLEUTNANT GÜNTHER GOEBEL

Günther Goebel was born in Hagen, Westphalia on 14 November 1917. He joined Infanterie Regiment 18 in Detmold on 1 April 1936 as a potential officer and, in 1937, attended the Dresden Kriegsschule and the Döberitz Infanterieschule, being commissioned as a Leutnant on 1 April 1938. He was initially posted as a platoon commander with 9 Kompanie, Infanterie Regiment 80, before transferring on 1 October 1938 to its 10 Kompanie.

By 1939, Goebel was Adjutant of 1 Bat./Infanterie Regiment 208 in the 79 Infanterie Division. The division first saw action on the Saar Front against French troops during 1939–40. In November 1939, Goebel was awarded the Iron Cross Second Class whilst serving on the Western Front. In June of the following year, during the German sweep through France, he was awarded the Iron Cross First Class as Company Commander of 3 Komp./Infanterie Regt 208 during the attack on Luneville. Shortly afterwards, he was appointed as Regimental Adjutant.

After the successful conclusion of the Balkan campaign, Goebel's division was part of VI Armee during the invasion of the Soviet Union. He took part in the crossing of the Bug near Sokal and fought in the Ukraine. The division took part in the Battle of Kiev where several Soviet armies were trapped. On 18 October 1941, Goebel was awarded the Knight's Cross for his part in leading the advance battalion *Von Wedel* when the supply routes to the Soviet forces were captured. On 6 November 1941, Goebel was entered into the Roll of Honour of the German Army.

February 1942 found Goebel promoted to Hauptmann and commander of 1 Infanterie Regiment 208 but, a few days later, he was severely wounded and spent two months in hospital recovering from his wounds. In May 1942,

SS-Brigadeführer Theodor Wisch wears the German Cross in Gold on the right breast pocket and the ribbon of the East Front Campaign medal in the buttonhole. On the left cuff is the 'Adolf Hitler' title of the Leibstandarte. (Theodor Wisch.)

Oberstleutnant Günther Goebel, in this photograph a Major, was awarded the Oakleaves in January 1943 as a Kampfgruppe commander on the Eastern Front. He was also decorated with the Honour Roll Clasp of the German army. (Günther Goebel.)

Goebel was appointed to Armee-Oberkommando VI in the Stalingrad area for training as a staff officer, then tasked with the formation of an Infantry Training School in the same area.

During December 1942, Goebel was in command of a Kampfgruppe in the area around Nishij and Tschiskaja on the Don bridgehead. On 18 January 1943, he became the 180th recipient of the Oakleaves for his successful command of the Kampfgruppe. Two weeks later, he was again severely wounded and returned to Germany for hospital treatment. On 7 February, he was promoted to Major. Goebel was back in action in time for the Kursk Offensive (Operation ZITADELLE) before being sent to the Kriegsakademie in Hirschberg, Silesia.

On 1 April 1944, Goebel was appointed to the staff of 62 Infanterie Division, Armeegruppe Nord, at Narva. Around this time he was also awarded the Close Combat Clasp in Silver. During the late summer of 1944, Major Goebel was appointed deputy Quartermaster of XXXIII ArmeeKorps, Armeegruppe Nord.

Over the end of 1944 and early 1945, Major Goebel served with both 218 and 215 Infanterie Divisions. On 1 March 1945, he was promoted to the rank of Oberstleutnant with 215 Infanterie Division in Courland, shortly before being appointed Regimental Commander with 183 Infanterie Regiment, 82 Infanterie Division. Two days before the German surrender, Oberstleutnant Goebel was captured and spent ten years in Soviet captivity.

OBERLEUTNANT EKKEHARD KYLLING-SCHMIDT

Born on 21 June 1918 in Flensburg, Ekkehard Kylling-Schmidt began his military career in October 1938 when he joined Infanterie Regiment 26, part of 18 Infanterie Division. He saw service as a Platoon Commander during the Polish Campaign and on the Western Front before being transferred to the Eastern Front where Infanterie Regt 26 was committed to Operation BARBAROSSA, the invasion of the Soviet Union. Kylling-Schmidt found himself serving as a Company Commander with 3 Kompanie of the regiment and was awarded the Knight's Cross for his command of the company during the early phases of the invasion. His award was made on 20 October 1941.

The regiment was amongst the units encircled in the Demjansk pocket and remained trapped for over a year before the successful break out. By this time, Kylling-Schmidt was an Oberleutnant and Commander of 4 Kompanie of the regiment. On 4 December 1942, whilst still trapped within the Demjansk pocket, he was awarded the Oakleaves for his command of the unit during the ferocious battles in the defence of the trapped army.

Oberleutnant Kylling-Schmidt remained with the regiment until October 1943 when he was seriously wounded and evacuated from the front. On his recovery, he was posted to the military Academy in Berlin for General Staff training. In May 1945, he was taken into captivity on the Western Front and was released in August of that year.

Ekkehard Kylling-Schmidt was a well-liked and respected officer. His personal gallantry was well known as was his proficiency in tank 'killing'.

SS-OBERSTURMBANNFÜHRER GERD BREMER

Born in Dusterntal in July 1917, Gerd Bremer joined the SS-Verfügungstruppe as a volunteer with the SS-Standarte *Germania* in October 1936. After attending the SS Junkerschule at Bad Tölz in Bavaria, Bremer was commissioned into the elite *Leibstandarte SS Adolf Hitler* as an SS-Untersturmführer in 1937.

Bremer took part in the Polish Campaign, winning the Iron Cross Second Class for actions around Warsaw. This was followed by the Iron Cross First Class during the course of the Western Campaign.

Moving East for the invasion of the Soviet Union, Bremer commanded the Kradschützenkompanie of the *Leibstandarte*. The very mobile nature of motorcycle troops meant that they were often to be found at the very forefront of the fighting and this was certainly the case with Bremer and his men. During these early days of the Eastern Campaign, Soviet forces were retreating faster than the Germans could advance. Bremer's unit raced after the retreating Soviets and in one single engagement captured over 500 prisoners and a hoard of military equipment. Bremer's unit stormed on through two Soviet defence lines and outflanked a third, penetrating into the enemy town of Mariupol. For his success in these early days of Operation BARBAROSSA, Bremer was decorated with the Knight's Cross on 30 October 1941.

As a Leutnant with 3 Kompanie, Infanterie Regiment 26 Ekkehard Kylling-Schmidt was decorated with the Knight's Cross in October 1941 for actions on the Eastern Front. (Author Collection.)

Oakleaves winner Generalleutnant Walter Fries wearing the old-style field cap with his General's service tunic. Fries later reached the rank of General der Panzertruppe.

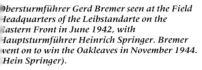

Obersturmführer Gerd Bremer seen at the Field Headquarters of the Leibstandarte on the Eastern Front in June 1942, with Hauptsturmführer Heinrich Springer. Bremer went on to win the Oakleaves in November 1944. (Hein Springer).

Bremer, photographed on the Eastern Front in the summer of 1942, wearing the rarely encountered white SS summer tunic. Note that the normal SS-style sleeve insignia is not being worn on this jacket. (Gerd Bremer.)

This impetuous daredevil attitude was to typify Bremer's style of leadership. Bremer remained with the Kradschützenkompanie on the Eastern Front, his reputation as a fearless daredevil continuing to grow. In 1943, Bremer was transferred to the newly formed 12 SS Panzer Division *Hitlerjugend* and given command of the division's Aufklärungsabteilung. The reckless bravery of the young grenadiers of *Hitlerjugend* is well known and Bremer's style of leadership was ideally suited to these fanatical young men.

During the hectic fighting after the Allied invasion of Normandy, Bremer was awarded the Close Combat Clasp in Silver. By the end of the first weeks in July, *Hitlerjugend* had suffered heavy casualties with 60 percent of the unit strength either dead, wounded or missing. Over half of the division's vehicle strength was lost. Caught in the Falaise cauldron, only a few *Hitlerjugend* fought their way out. Bremer was decorated as the 668th recipient of the Oakleaves on 25 November 1944 in recognition of his command of the Aufklärungsabteilung in Normandy.

In the meantime, in September, the division had been reformed and brought up to strength for use in Hitler's final gamble in the West, the Ardennes offensive. Bremer served with the unit during that offensive and saw action in Hungary before surrendering with the remnants of the division to US forces in Austria. Shortly before the surrender, Bremer had been promoted to SS-Obersturmbannführer.

This charismatic daredevil survived the war and now lives in Spain, having moved there after his release from French captivity in 1947.

GENERAL DER PANZERTRUPPE WALTER FRIES

Walter Fries was born on 22 April 1894 in Gustenhain. He served in the German army during World War One, being commissioned in 1915, and saw post-war service in the Police. In October 1936, Fries rejoined the army and was given command of 2/Infanterie Regiment 15, with the rank of Major. In 1938, he was promoted to Oberstleutnant.

After service in the Polish and French campaigns, summer 1940 found Fries as the commander of 87 Infanterie Regiment (Mot.) It was in this capacity that, on 14 December 1941, he was decorated with the Knight's Cross for his part in the success of the regiment whilst part of Heeresgruppe Nord during the opening phases of Operation BARBAROSSA.

Fries then served for a short period as the Head of Instruction at Dresden Infantry School before being appointed, in March 1943, to command the recently formed 29 Panzer Grenadier Division. The unit fought in Sicily and during the Italian campaign at Salerno and Anzio. In January 1944, Fries was decorated with the Oakleaves for his successful command of the division during the Italian campaign. The Swords followed in August of the same year.

In December 1944, Fries was promoted to the rank of General der Panzertruppe and ended the war as Commanding General of XXXVI Panzer Korps. Fries, an able and respected commander, survived the war and died in Weilburg in August 1982 at the age of 88.

1942
THE TURNING POINT

The beginning of 1942 found the German forces on the Eastern Front being pushed back, with three entire divisions destroyed to the south west of Moscow. Stalin ordered a general offensive along the whole central sector of the front. By 14 January, Russian spearheads were only 14 kilometres from Kharkov.

In March, the Red Army counter-attacked in the Crimea and the German Armies continued to struggle throughout the entire Eastern Front. By the end of the month, only eight out of 162 German divisions were at full strength. Since the opening of Operation *Barbarossa*, German losses were over one million dead, wounded or missing. Russian losses, however, were over seven million. Russia, though, was a vast enough country to absorb even such appalling losses as these. Germany, on the other hand, was beginning to find it difficult to replace its losses.

During May, German forces on the Eastern Front regained the initiative despite a Russian counter-offensive on the south west sector. On 23 May, Panzer spearheads trapped two Soviet armies in the Barvenkovo Salient capturing nearly a quarter of a million prisoners. By the end of the month, German forces were still pushing back the Russians and as the summer wore on, the German 6 Army was approaching Stalingrad and Kleist's Panzers were crossing the River Don. By August, the Germans had taken the Caucasus with its great oil wealth, essential to the war effort.

Throughout September and October, von Paulus launched several major efforts to capture Stalingrad despite extreme resistance from the Soviet defenders, determined to fight to the last man and the last bullet. By the end of October, things at Stalingrad were beginning to become serious for von Paulus as Zhukov launched a surprise counter-offensive, encircling 6 Army. Göring boasted to Hitler that the *Luftwaffe* could keep the encircled German troops supplied by air, but, despite heroic efforts by his transport flyers, Göring's *Luftwaffe* could only supply around 20 percent of the basic minimum requirements of 6 Army. As the army settled in to await the horrors of a Russian winter as the year drew to a close, with totally inadequate food, equipment and ammunition, surrounded by overwhelmingly superior Soviet forces, Hoth and von Manstein attempted to break through the encirclement, but without success.

The year started better for the German forces in North Africa, as Rommel captured Agedabia and re-took Benghazi at the end of January. Both Rommel and Kesselring agreed that the British-held island of Malta must be neutralised to prevent British air strikes against German supply routes but despite furious attacks, Malta remained undefeated. On land, Rommel's offensive continued, though somewhat slowed by lack of supplies, until 21 June, when Tobruk fell with thirty-two thousand Allied prisoners. With Tobruk taken, Rommel

Above left: Leutnant Adolf Schmahl won the Knight's Cross on the Eastern Front in July 1942 whilst serving with 10 Kompanie, Infanterie Regiment 6. (Adolf Schmahl)

Above right: Admiral Kurt Fricke was awarded the Knight's Cross in October 1942 as a Staff Officer for his part in the successful planning of naval operations. (Josef Charita)

Two veteran NCO's of the elite **Grossdeutschland** *Division, Oberfeldwebel Klemm of the Infanterie Regiment, and Oberfeldwebel Wegner of the Sturmgeschutz Abteilung. (Chris Ailsby)*

pushed on and by 1 July, had reached El Alamein. The Afrika Korps had advanced over 600 kilometres in just 36 days.

Despite these victories, supplies were a constant problem for Rommel and this factor combined with the stout defence put up by Auchinleck's soldiers, halted Rommel at the gates of El Alamein.

On the evening of 23 October, the British 8 Army launched its counter-offensive, preceded by an artillery bombardment by almost one thousand guns. The weeks that followed saw the Afrika Korps, weakened by lack of fuel and equipment, slowly forced back through Libya to the Tunisian border. German losses in dead and wounded exceeded ten thousand, and over 300 irreplaceable tanks were lost. It was the beginning of the end for Rommel's desert army.

At sea, the year began with Operation PAUKENSCHLAG as Dönitz's U-boats carried the war to the east coast of the United States. In just under one month, 20 Allied ships were sunk by just four U-boats. During the following month this success continued with a further 70 Allied vessels sent to the bottom, mostly valuable oil tankers.

Hitler's *Kriegsmarine* also provided him with a great propaganda boost for the nation's morale when the battlecruisers *Scharnhorst* and *Gneisenau* succeeded in breaking through the English Channel in the so-called 'Channel Dash'. *Gneisenau*, however, was so badly damaged in a bombing raid shortly after the successful breakthrough that she was decommissioned in July.

Despite rising losses, Dönitz's U-boats continued to score successes against Allied shipping. In July, 23 out of 36 merchantmen from Convoy PQ17 had been destroyed. The Convoy had scattered, fearing attack by German surface raiders, and the stragglers had become easy prey in one of the war's worst convoy defeats for the Allies. On 11 August, the British aircraft carrier *Eagle* was sunk by *U-73*. U-boat successes continued throughout the year with a total of 750,000 tons of shipping sunk in November alone.

During 1942, bombing raids carried out by the RAF were beginning to have a serious effect on the German war economy and on civilian morale. In May, the first of the RAF's Thousand Bomber Raids was mounted on Cologne. RAF bombers dropped over 1,400 tons of bombs. More than five thousand people died in just one night. On 1 June, it was the turn of Essen and on 25 June, Bremen suffered the same fate.

1942 had been a year of changing fortunes for Germany but in the main it had been able to hold its own. The year's end, however, saw defeat looming on two fronts. Massive losses were now becoming more and more difficult to make up and from now on, although Germany would score many minor victories and launch several successful counter-attacks on a localised basis on various fronts, its fate was sealed. From 1943 onwards, despite the bravest efforts of German soldiers on all fronts, ultimate defeat was inevitable.

During 1942, a total of approximately 952 Knight's Crosses was awarded, 110 sets of Oakleaves and eighteen Swords.

SS-STURMBANNFÜHRER HEINRICH SPRINGER

Heinrich Springer was born on 3 November 1914 in Eckernförde, Kiel, the son of an officer in the *Kaiserliche Marine*. Wishing to become a construction engineer, he attended the Technical High School in Eckernförde before volunteering for the SS in 1937. Springer was accepted into the SS-Verfügungstruppe and served with the *Germania* and *Der Führer* Standarten, seeing service during the annexation of Austria and the occupation of the Sudetenland. In November 1938, he commenced officer training at the SS Junkerschule at Bad Tölz in Bavaria. Springer passed his course with good marks and was commissioned into the elite *Leibstandarte Adolf Hitler* as an SS-Untersturmführer in October 1939.

During the German invasion of France and the Low Countries, Springer served as a platoon commander, winning the Iron Cross Second Class during the advance on Dunkirk. During the course of this campaign, Springer also received the Infantry Assault Badge and the Wound Badge in black for his first wound received in action. Promoted to the rank of SS-Obersturmführer in September 1940, Springer also served in both the Greek and Jugoslavian campaigns before the commencement of Operation BARBAROSSA in 1941.

During July 1941, whilst serving as Adjutant to 1 Bat./LSSAH, Springer led a combat patrol deep behind enemy lines to establish contact with III Armee Korps under General von Mackensen which had been isolated from the rest of the German forces. This mission was achieved with total success and no losses. Having established contact, the patrol was sent out once again to inform their beleaguered comrades of the plans to link up. Once again this mission was carried out with total success and no casualties. For this achievement, Springer was decorated with the Iron Cross First Class by the Divisional Commander, Josef 'Sepp' Dietrich.

In November 1941, the *Leibstandarte* was committed to the attack on Rostov. Heinrich Springer, by now an SS-Hauptsturmführer, was in command of 3 Kompanie of the LSSAH. On 20 November, Springer and his men reached the River Don and found that a bridge over the river was still intact although Soviet engineers had set demolition charges. Springer spotted an enemy locomotive nearby with a full head of steam up and had his men open fire on it. As the high pressure steam escaped from a myriad holes, Springer took advantage of the total confusion amongst the enemy and he and his men stormed onto the bridge.

In the mêlée which followed, Springer's men managed to remove the demolition charges and, despite furious Soviet attempts to dislodge them, held the bridge until reinforcements could arrive and consolidate the position. The capture of this bridge intact was instrumental in the crossing of the Don. If the bridge had been demolished and the *Leibstandarte's* engineers had to construct a crossing under enemy fire, losses would have been considerable. With the *Leibstandarte* over the river, the fighting moved on into Rostov itself.

On the day following the crossing, Springer was seriously wounded and had to be evacuated to a hospital in Berlin for treatment. Whilst recuperating in hospital, Springer was visited by the *Leibstandarte's* Commanding Officer, 'Sepp' Dietrich and presented with the *Urkunde* for his Knight's Cross, officially awarded on 12 January 1942 for his achievement in capturing the Don bridge.

On his recovery, Hauptsturmführer Springer returned to the front in May 1942, joining the *Leibstandarte* at Taganrog, where he took command of 1 Kompanie. He saw continuous action until March 1943 when, during the severe fighting at Kharkov, he was struck in the head by splinters from an exploding enemy tank shell, and once again evacuated to a military hospital. Springer was promoted to the rank of SS-Sturmbannführer whilst recover-

Hein Springer in the black pre-war uniform as a new member of SS-Standarte 2 Germania. (Hein Springer.)

Hauptsturmführer Springer shortly after the award of his Knight's Cross on 12 January 1942. (Hein Springer.)

Springer as a newly commissioned SS-Untersturmführer of the elite Leibstandarte

with his wife Ursula on their wedding day in December 1939. (Hein Springer.)

67

Springer, third from left, front row, with the assembled officers of the 12 SS Panzer Division Hitlerjugend in 1944. Next to Springer, from *left to right, are Kurt 'Panzer' Meyer, Max Wünsche and Fritz Witt, all former members of the Leibstandarte. (Munin Verlag.)*

Sturmbannführer Springer (with field cap and briefcase) with Generalfeldmarschall Model as Model's Ordnance Officer. Model is conversing *with Paratroop General Eugen Meindl. (Hein Springer)*

ing from his wounds. When fit for duty once again, he was posted to the newly formed 12 SS Panzer Division *Hitlerjugend* as Divisional Adjutant. Springer was just one of several combat-experienced *Leibstandarte* personnel transferred to the new division to instil the typical fighting spirit of the Waffen-SS in the new young grenadiers of *Hitlerjugend*.

In August 1944, Springer was appointed First Ordnance Officer on the staff of the commander of Armee Gruppe 'B' on the Western Front, Generalfeldmarschall Walter Model. Springer saw action at Arnhem during the ill-fated British airborne attempt to capture the Arnhem bridge. He remained on Model's staff until the end of the war, when he was taken into British captivity.

Held in high regard by both his subordinates and his superiors, Springer's personal gallantry is well attested by his decorations which include the Rumanian Order of the Star and the Bulgarian Order of Military Virtue.

After the war Springer returned to his pre-war vocation of constructional engineering. He built himself a beautiful home in his native Schleswig-Holstein where he lives today in retirement.

Heinrich Springer has given considerable assistance in the assembling of much of the information used in both this work and the author's *The Iron Cross — A History 1813–1957*, also published by Blandford Press.

KORVETTENKAPITÄN REINHARD HARDEGEN

Born in Bremen on 18 March 1913, Reinhard Hardegen joined the *Reichsmarine* in 1933 at the age of 20. He served on the sail-trainer *Gorch Fock* and on the Cruiser *Karlsruhe*, seeing most of the world on numerous goodwill cruises.

On 1 November 1939, he was sent to U-boat school and after training, was posted as First Officer of *U-124*. After a year's experience in a front-line U-boat, Hardegen was given his own command, in December 1940, *U-147*, a Type IID vessel of the 1st U-Flotille. As a Kapitänleutnant with his own command, Hardegen scored his first success when he sunk a 9,000-ton steamer in the North Sea.

Hardegen subsequently was transferred to the command of *U-123*, a Type IXB U-boat operating from Lorient with 2 U-Flotille. *U-123* was a 'lucky ship' whose previous commander had been awarded the Knight's Cross for his successful command of her, operating in the mid-Atlantic. It was to prove a successful ship for Hardegen, too, and his score on his first voyage with her was 30,000 tons of enemy shipping.

In further operations in the North Sea, *U-123* sank the British auxiliary cruiser *Aurania*. His real successes, however, were to come with the entry of the United States into the war. The rich pickings along the US coastline were now legitimate targets for Dönitz's U-boats. From 12 to 29 January 1942, Hardegen in *U-123* sank nine ships totalling over 53,000 tons. In recognition of his success, he was decorated with the Knight's Cross on 23 January 1942.

After a brief return to port in February 1942, Hardegen was back in action off the US coast in March and once again had a very successful time of it, sinking in excess of 79,000 tons of enemy shipping. For this, he was decorated with the

Oakleaves on 23 April 1942. Hardegen received a congratulatory telegram reading:

Kapitänleutnant Hardegen is awarded, as the 89th soldier, the Oakleaves to the Knight's Cross of the Iron Cross. A well deserved decoration and honour for the Commander and crew of *U-123*.

These actions off the American Coast were to be the most successful of all Germany's U-boat triumphs.

In autumn 1944, Hardegen was removed from active sea service. As the tide turned in the U-boat war, too many U-boats and their crews were not returning. Experienced commanders such as Hardegen were too valuable to risk losing in action. Their knowledge could be used to train and inform novice U-boat commanders, promoting their greater success and perhaps survival, or to advise on tactics, equipment and weapons. Consequently, in October 1944, Hardegen was posted to the Torpedo Weapons Inspectorate of the Oberkommando der Wehrmacht.

However, in the final months of the war, Hardegen was given command of a marine infantry batallion in a marine infantry division. These units were formed at the very end of the war from sailors who no longer had ships in which to serve. Many U-boat men found themselves serving in such infantry units in the closing days of the war.

Reinhard Hardegen survived the war and now lives in retirement in Bremen.

HAUPTMANN HANS JOACHIM MARSEILLE

A Berliner, born in December 1919, Hans Joachim Marseille was to become one of the *Luftwaffe*'s most famous fighter pilots before his untimely death in 1942. He commenced his career with the *Luftwaffe* at the age of eighteen, in October 1938, and first saw action in the Western Campaign in 1940. He soon achieved his first victories but his comrades and superiors could hardly have foreseen his later legendary successes, as Marseille himself was shot down four times in the course of gaining his first seven victories. In September 1940, during the Battle of Britain, Marseille was awarded the Iron Cross First Class.

In March 1941, young officer candidate Marseille arrived in North Africa and his amazing success story soon began. Commissioned as a Leutnant in June 1941, he was awarded the German Cross in Gold in December of that year. By February 1942, he had reached a score of 50 victories and was awarded the Knight's Cross on 22 February. On 3 June, he shot down six enemy aircraft within only eleven minutes. Within three days, Marseille's score stood at 75 and he was awarded the Oakleaves on 6 June.

Shortly after the award of the Oakleaves, Marseille displayed his skill once again when on 17 June, he once again shot down six enemy aircraft during a single engagement, this time taking only seven minutes! Such was his proficiency and his amazing marksmanship that within twelve days of being

Korvettenkapitän Reinhard Hardegen. The Oakleaves are shown to particular advantage in this exceptionally fine portrait study of one of Germany's greatest U-boat aces. Hardegen sank over 66,000 tons of enemy shipping in one single voyage. (Reinhard Hardegen)

Hauptmann Hans Joachim Marseille, the 'Star of Africa'. This photograph shows young Marseille as an Oberleutnant, wearing the tropical Luftwaffe tunic. Only the shoulder straps indicate rank on this type of tunic. This photograph was taken shortly after the award of the Diamonds. (Luftwaffen Museum, Uetersen)

awarded the Oakleaves, his score had risen to 101, bringing the award of the Swords on 18 June, only twelve days after the award of the Oakleaves.

Marseille's skill at the 'multiple kill' was fast becoming legendary. On 1 September 1942, he shot down seventeen RAF fighters in just three sorties, all on the same day. Of these seventeen kills, eight were made within the space of just ten minutes. Marseille became the fourth recipient of the Swords, Oakleaves and Diamonds on 2 September 1942, after his 126th victory. His score is all the more impressive when one considers that every victory was scored on the Western Front — West Europe and the Desert — against well-trained and equipped adversaries.

Shortly after the award of his Diamonds, Marseille again scored one of his celebrated multiple kills, when, on 15 September, he shot down seven enemy aircraft within just eleven minutes. Two weeks later, Marseille was returning from a mission when his Bf 109 fighter developed engine trouble. Marseille was forced to bale out but as he did so, he was struck by the tailplane of his aircraft and killed outright. Marseille, the 'Star of Africa', died on 30 September 1942, at the age of only 22. He had already reached the rank of Hauptmann and held the highest decorations his country could bestow.

Hauptmann Marseille's Diamonds are on display at the Luftwaffen Museum at Uetersen along with several other of his personal effects. A visit to this superb museum is highly recommended to anyone visiting Northern Germany.

SS-Hauptsturmführer Wilfried Richter is wearing the SS version of the Field Grey assault gun tunic with the Deaths Head Divisional insignia on both collar patches. In this case, only the shoulder straps indicated rank. The Totenkopf on his old style field cap appears to be cut from a collar patch as it faces the opposite direction to the normal cap badge. (Heinz Macher)

Oakleaves winner Helmut Hudel, shown here wearing the black Panzer jacket and field cap. The officers version of the field cap has silver piping to the crown and the scallop at the front. The national emblem is in silver wire weave. (Helmut Hudel)

SS-HAUPTSTURMFÜHRER WILFRIED RICHTER

Wilfried Richter was born in May 1916 in Pforzheim, the son of a local businessman. Joining the SS in 1937, he was accepted into 15 Kompanie/SS Standarte *Deutschland*. After attending SS Junkerschule, he was attached to the SS *Totenkopf* Division. During the invasion of the Soviet Union both Second and First Class Iron Crosses were awarded to Richter in late 1941.

His division, however, was one of the major units cut off in the Demjansk pocket in the northern sector of the Eastern Front. From February through to April of 1942, *Totenkopf* units came under continuous heavy Soviet artillery bombardment which reduced their area to a sea of rubble. In mid-April, Richter took command of a strongpoint in the sector which had suffered particularly from the enemy bombardment and was quick to organise the construction and strengthening of defensive positions against impending attack.

A further Soviet attack soon materialised, supported by sixteen T-34 tanks, and succeeded in establishing a hold on part of the German positions. *Totenkopf*'s anti-tank weapons managed to destroy six of the attacking tanks before being knocked out. Further daring attacks by *Totenkopf* grenadiers eliminated a further five tanks by the use of 'Teller' mines.

Richter arranged a barrage of *Totenkopf*'s remaining artillery on the Soviet-held area during which a further T-34 was knocked out. Gathering all the remaining grenadiers around him, Richter stormed into the Soviet-held area, engaging the enemy in furious hand to hand combat. The enemy suffered heavy losses and were eventually thrown back. In recognition of this achievement, Richter was awarded the Knight's Cross on 21 April 1942.

Richter also saw service with the *schwere* Kompanie of SS Panzer Regiment 3 before being attached to the SS Junkerschule at Bad Tölz as an instructor. Ultimately, Richter became a deputy Regimental Commander in 38 SS Panzer Grenadier Division *Nibelungen*. This unit was formed at the end of the war from the staff and trainees at the various SS Junkerschulen. It fought briefly in Bavaria before surrendering to US troops in May 1945.

Richter survived the war but after a long illness died in 1981.

MAJOR HELMUT HUDEL

Born in July 1915 in Raunheim, Hudel's military career began in 1934 when he volunteered for service and was accepted into Kraftfahrabteilung 5. After attending military academy, he was commissioned as a Leutnant in 1936, joining Panzer Regiment 7. In 1938, he was attached to the Kriegsschule in Potsdam, where he remained until 1940, rejoining Panzer Regiment 7, then part of 10 Panzer Division. The division was sent to Russia in June 1941 and saw action at Minsk and Smolensk.

Promoted to Hauptmann in March 1942, Hudel was decorated with the Knight's Cross on 27 May of that year whilst detached to a Kampfgruppe of the 20 Panzer Division in the central sector of the Eastern Front around Wjasma. 10 Panzer Division had been so badly mauled in this fighting that it was withdrawn from front-line duties and sent to France to rest and refit.

In late 1942, the division was sent to Tunisia in an attempt to counter the Allied landings there, thrown into the fighting in an attempt to hold the expanding Allied bridgehead. The years of victory for Rommel's once mighty Afrika Korps were over. By April 1943, the division was part of a general retreat away from the advancing Allies. Hudel received the Oakleaves on 2 April 1943 in recognition of his service in commanding 1 Abteilung of Panzer Regiment 7 during the defensive actions in Tunisia. However, by 21 April, the division had only 25 tanks left. It surrendered to US forces on 9 May 1945. However, Hudel had been transferred from the African theatre before the end.

In 1944, Hudel was given command of the army's *schwere* Panzer Abteilung 508, equipped with the formidable Tiger tank, in Italy. Later that year, he was appointed to command the reserve tank training Abteilung of the elite *Grossdeutschland* Panzer Division. He remained with this unit until February 1945 when he was given command of *Panzer Lehr* Regiment which fought in Holland in March 1945 and later tried to squash the US bridgehead at Remagen. By the end of this battle, the once mighty *Panzer Lehr* was a burnt out shell, with only fifteen tanks left, and surrendered to US forces in the Ruhr pocket.

Helmut Hudel survived the war, and died in 1985 at the age of 69.

OBERSTLEUTNANT KARL-HEINZ OESTERWIRTZ

Born in Innsbruck in Austria in March 1914, Karl-Heinz Oesterwirtz initially served with Infanterie Regiment 150 before joining the Infanterie Lehr Regiment für besonderen Verwendung, the famous Brandenburgers. They were probably the nearest thing the *Wehrmacht* had to today's SAS, and they often operated behind enemy lines, dressed in enemy uniforms, sowing confusion and fear. The importance of *Brandenburg*'s contribution to the war effort may be reflected in the fact that during a single campaign, the French, over 75 per cent of the Regiment's strength was awarded the Iron Cross.

A daring and reliable officer, Oesterwirtz commanded 7 Kompanie of the Regiment on the Eastern Front. On 11 August 1942, Oberleutnant Oesterwirtz, in classic *Brandenburg* style, had captured a Russian held bridge near Belorelschkaja by subterfuge, using captured enemy vehicles to approach undetected. For this achievement he was awarded the Knight's Cross of the Iron Cross. As the war progressed, however, *Brandenburg* was used more and more as a regular combat unit, its commando style operations declining in direct proportion to the fading influence of the Abwehr at Hitler's Headquarters.

Brandenburg was moved from the Eastern Front to the Balkans in 1943 and then, in 1944, it was moved to Vienna. There it reformed as a Panzer grenadier division before returning to the Eastern Front, where it served with 4 Panzer Armee as a component unit of the elite Panzerkorps *Grossdeutschland*. Once masters of the covert Commando type operation, the Brandenburgers were to spend the remaining months of the war fighting as conventional infantry in an attempt to stem the inexorable Soviet advance. On 11/12 February 1945, Oesterwirtz rescued a German supply column from an enemy occupied area around Sprottau and for this the intrepid officer became the 743rd recipient of the Oakleaves.

Karl Heinz Oesterwirtz survived the war and is still alive.

SS-STANDARTENFÜHRER JOHANNES MÜHLENKAMP

A native of Metz, Johannes Mühlenkamp was born on 9 October 1910 and joined the SS-Verfügungstruppe in 1934, being accepted into the *Germania* Standarte. After attending the SS Junkerschule at Braunschweig, he was commissioned as an SS-Untersturmführer. In 1938, he was given command of 15 SS-Kradschützenkompanie of the *Germania* Standarte. Mühlenkamp served with this unit during the Polish Campaign and was one of the first soldiers to win both Second and First Class Iron Crosses of 1939.

Throughout the Western Campaign, he served as an adjutant to Paul Hausser who was impressed by his military skills and gave him command of the Aufklärungsabteilung of the SS-Verfügungsdivision. Mühlenkamp commanded his troops with great élan during the Balkan campaign and the

Oberstleutnant Karl-Heinz Oesterwirtz. This rare photograph shows the Brandenburg sleeve band on the right cuff. Photographic evidence of this band being worn is very rare indeed. Note also the Jäger sleeve badge of an oakleaves spray and the cloth version of the German Cross in Gold. (Karl-Heinz Oesterwirtz)

SS-Standartenführer Johannes Mühlenkamp. It is interesting to note that Mühlenkamp's SS Officers Cap bears an army officers embroidered cap eagle in place of the standard SS pattern. This was a fairly common occurrence when supplies were scarce. (Johannes Mühlenkamp)

opening phases of the invasion of the Soviet Union. A born soldier, his qualities were quickly recognised by his superiors. He was wounded in action several times and when in hospital recovering from wounds in June 1942, he was awarded the German Cross in Gold.

As the Waffen-SS expanded, it was decided to add a Panzer Abteilung to its strength. It was initially intended that this should go to the *Das Reich* Division but it was assigned to the *Wiking* Division. The command was given to Mühlenkamp. The success of the attack on Rostov during late summer 1942, was due in no small measure to Mühlenkamp's skilled command of his tanks during the battle, and for his command of the Panzer Abteilung during the attack Mühlenkamp was awarded the Knight's Cross. The award was made on 3 September 1942.

The Abteilung was eventually expanded to regimental strength, with Mühlenkamp still in command. The *Wiking* Division was fast gaining a reputation as one of the best units in the Waffen-SS. In the space of just one month, from 4 August to 3 September 1944, the division added 150 enemy tanks, nineteen assault guns, thirteen self-propelled guns and armoured cars and five enemy aircraft to its credit. Soviet units were never happy to find themselves up against *Wiking* and on many occasions Soviet units many times numerically superior were given a bloody nose by this elite unit. In recognition of his continued skilled leadership of the Panzer Regiment, on 21 September 1944, Mühlenkamp was awarded the Oakleaves. Unlike many of his contemporaries, who saw service with a number of units as they progressed through the rank structure, Mühlenkamp remained with his division. A true 'Wikinger' the name of Johannes Mühlenkamp will always be linked with the division whose success was in no small measure due to his skills as a soldier. On 9 October 1944, the Divisional Commander, General Gille, was promoted to command IV SS Panzer Korps, and command of 5 SS Panzer Division *Wiking* passed to Mühlenkamp.

Mühlenkamp's ultimate posting was as Inspector General of Waffen-SS Panzertruppe. Reaching the rank of Standartenführer, Mühlenkamp survived the war and is still alive.

LEUTNANT HANS STURM

Hans Sturm was born in Dortmund on 29 July 1920, the son of an engineer. After leaving school, he studied metal working and attended both day and night classes at the State Engineering Schools in Dortmund and Aachen. Sturm was called up for military service in October 1940, joining an infantry reserve unit in Herford. On 29 October, he was posted to Infanterie Regiment 473, part of 253 Infanterie Division, joining the unit in France where it was part of the German army of occupation. The unit remained in France until it was transferred to Poland in the spring of 1941 in preparation for the invasion of the Soviet Union.

The division entered Russia in June 1941 and took part in the assault on Moscow. Within a few weeks, Sturm had seen a considerable amount of action and was awarded the Iron Cross Second Class on 29 July, and the First Class only three days later on 1 August. On 22 August, Sturm was wounded in action by grenade splinters during close combat action. However, he received the first of a number of battlefield promotions when he was made up to Gefreiter on 1 September.

In December 1941, Sturm qualified for the Infantry Assault Badge. Early in 1942 he received the campaign medal for the Winter Battles in the East (Medaille Winterschlacht im Osten). During this period the division had fought in numerous defensive battles against the Soviet winter offensive, and in January had been encircled south of Lake Volga, only managing to break out with heavy casualties. Sturm was decorated with the German Cross in Gold on 26 August 1942, though it was not presented until November of that year.

In early September 1942, the division was located in the Volga bridgehead near Rzev. During the night of 13/14 September, a Soviet attack was launched against the German positions. One strategically positioned machine-gun nest was instrumental in holding back the Soviet attackers until it received a direct hit. Sturm immediately realised the serious situation caused by the loss of the weapon and ran to the position. Finding the weapon undamaged he immediately opened fire on the advancing enemy and once again threw them back, but his position came under heavy enemy fire.

Gefreiter Hans Sturm, after the presentation of his Knight's Cross in the field hospital at Smolensk. Sturm still wears an eye patch over his injured right eye. He had not yet received his German Cross in Gold at this point. (Hans Sturm)

By the time this photograph was taken in Aachen in 1943, Sturm had been promoted to Unteroffizier and had received the German Cross in Gold, worn on the right breast pocket. This was not received until after the Knight's Cross. (Hans Sturm)

The Soviets were determined to neutralise this machine-gun nest, knowing that with its removal their chances of success would be much greater. With the weight of enemy fire being directed on to his position, it was only a matter of time before he would be hit. A huge explosion rocked his position and knocked Sturm unconscious. When he came to, he was suffering from a terrible head wound and had been blinded in the right eye by metal splinters. Despite his dreadful injuries, Sturm dragged himself back to his machine-gun and once again opened fire, driving off the attackers. Eventually, the attack was beaten off and Sturm was evacuated to a field hospital in Smolensk.

Whilst recuperating in hospital, he was awarded the Wound Badge in Silver and learned that he was to be decorated with the Knight's Cross for his gallantry. The award was made official on 26 September and on 4 October, the Knight's Cross was hung around Sturm's neck at the Smolensk hospital. Sturm was also promoted to Unteroffizier.

After recovering from his wounds, Unteroffizier Sturm was posted to the regimental reserve in Aachen. Sturm remained with the regimental reserve for a year, giving talks in the Wehrkreis area on front-line life and acting as a careers adviser for officers and NCO candidates.

In February 1944, Sturm was posted to 356 Infanterie Division, serving with 871 Infanterie Regiment where his engineering background was put to good use in the construction of defensive positions on the Italian Front. On 25

This photograph dates from August 1944 when Sturm was an Oberfeldwebel at the Kriegsschule in Hagenau. The braid slides at the base of his shoulder straps indicate his status as an officer aspirant. (Hans Sturm)

Taken one month after the previous photograph, this shot shows Sturm after his commissioning as a Leutnant wearing the officer quality embroidered badges on the peaked cap and the silver braid chin cords. Compare this to the NCO's cap held by Sturm on the preceding photograph. (Hans Sturm)

February 1944, he was promoted to Fahnenjunkerfeldwebel. He remained in Italy until May 1944 when he was transferred to Reserve Grenadier Regiment 88 in Fulda.

In June 1944, Sturm attended the military academy at Hagenau and was commissioned as a Leutnant on 1 September, and sent back to Reserve Grenadier Battaillon 88 until November 1944, when he was posted to Grafenwohr. Here, a course for Volksturm officers was being organised and Sturm's experience was put to good use in training the future officers of Germany's 'Peoples Army'.

Following this, in February 1945, Leutnant Sturm was given a special commission to serve on the Leadership Staff of the Volkssturm and saw action in the final battle for Berlin. Severely wounded in action again, he qualified for, but never received the Wound Badge in Gold.

At the age of 24, Hans Sturm went into Soviet captivity on 2 May 1945 and did not return until October 1953. After his release, Hans Sturm was employed as a technician until his retirement in 1980.

Hans Sturm is a modest and unassuming man. In a letter to the author he denied his gallantry and puts his Knight's Cross winning action down to the anger and desperation of the moment, and most of all, soldier's good luck.

1943
THE YEAR OF RETREAT

The beginning of 1943 saw the Russians launch their general winter counter-offensive on the Eastern Front and re-enter the Caucasus. By the middle of January, the Soviets had recaptured Kharkov through a counter-offensive in this area but von Manstein recaptured the town. On 21 January, the Russians captured Gumrak airfield, cutting off Stalingrad's last lifeline, and by the end of the month, von Paulus had been forced to surrender his forces in the south of Stalingrad. Two days later, the forces in the north surrendered also. The entire 6 Army was lost and Germany had suffered a dreadful blow both to its morale and its military power.

The Red Army once again captured Kharkov in February and in March re-captured Demjansk but were again thrown back at Kharkov. In the spring, the thaw on the Eastern Front had turned the countryside into a sea of mud and prevented much action by either side. Both the Soviets and the Germans had taken advantage of the opportunity for a much needed rest.

During June, Hitler's armies on the Eastern Front prepared themselves for the massive armoured punch at Kursk. Launched on 5 July, it was to be the biggest tank battle in history as nearly one million men and two and a half thousand tanks were thrown at the Soviets. However, thanks to Russian spy rings operating in Germany, the Red Army was well prepared for the assault. Although the German attack got off to a good start, a Soviet counter-offensive launched at Orel halted the Germans and the Kursk offensive was called off on 13 July.

In August, Orel and Bjelgorod fell to the Red Army at the start of the month, and as the month drew to a close, Kharkov fell to the Russians once again and Soviet troops went on to the offensive in the Ukraine.

The last quarter of 1943 was equally disastrous. In September, both Bryansk and Smolensk were lost, in November the Red Army took Kiev and in December, Cherkassy and Zhitomir fell to the Soviets.

Rommel's forces in North Africa were faring little better in 1943. Montgomery's Eighth Army had taken Tripoli in January, and in February Rommel launched Operation FRÜHLINGSWIND. This operation caused initial panic in the inexperienced American formations against which it was directed but the offensive quickly ran out of steam. A subsequent armoured attack on the Eighth Army's positions at Medenine was a costly failure; by now *Panzerarmee Afrika* was but a shadow of its former self. Rommel was recalled to Europe and command of German forces in Africa fell to Generaloberst von Arnim. The end in Africa came quickly as the British broke through the Mareth line at the end of March and the Wadi Akarit line in early April. On 12 May, von Arnim surrendered and over a quarter of a million German prisoners were taken. A further one hundred thousand had been lost during the North African campaign. Only a few hundred German troops escaped to Sicily.

The Allies, however, were not far behind and on 10 July, launched their invasion of Sicily. As the Germans started their fighting retreat towards the Straits of Messina, the Allies were to discover that the Germans, despite their morale-sapping defeat in North Africa, could still put up a strong defence. The German fighting spirit was by no means gone and some powerful formations were available for this masterly tactical retreat, including the elite *Hermann Göring* Division. The Allies had to fight for every inch of the way and the advance cost them dearly. When Sicily finally fell to the Allies on 17 August, many German troops had succeeded in crossing to safety in Italy. These troops were to be vital to the Germans when the Allied invasion of Italy commenced in September.

On 3 September, Allied forces landed on the Italian mainland at Calabria and, on 9 September, at Salerno. Despite the problems faced by the German High Command in Italy with the Italians negotiating an armistice with the Allies, a powerful enough force was organised to bring the Allied landings at Salerno to near disaster. Kesselring then carried out yet another successful fighting retreat to the Gustav line and Monte Cassino.

Germany's U-boats under Grossadmiral Dönitz had continued to take their toll of Allied shipping but these successes were only achieved with a heavy cost in U-boats sunk as Allied anti-submarine measures improved dramatically, so much so that on 24 May, Dönitz ordered a halt to his U-boat attacks on convoys. In the space of just two months, 56 U-boats had been lost. Allied technology had advanced to the degree that U-boats were now easy pickings. Ill-luck dogged the *Kriegsmarine* in 1943 and on 26 December, the battlecruiser *Scharnhorst* was sent to the bottom during the Battle of North Cape. The *Kriegsmarine* had lost a total of 237 U-boats during 1943 and, although over three million tons of Allied shipping had been destroyed, U-boat losses were now fast outstripping new production.

On the home front, RAF bombing raids continued to devastate the German cities. From 24 July to 2 August, in a series of bombing raids on Hamburg, over seventy nine thousand civilians had died.

A total of 1398 Knight's Crosses were awarded during 1943, with 187 Oakleaves and nineteen Swords.

OBERSTLEUTNANT MARTIN STEGLICH

Martin Steglich was born in Breslau on 16 July 1915. He joined Fusilier Regiment 27 in the Baltic port of Rostock on 1 October 1936 at the age of 21 and was commissioned as a Leutnant on 1 April 1939.

During the Polish Campaign, Leutnant Steglich was awarded the Iron Cross Second Class on 12 September 1939. The following year whilst on service on the Western Front, he received the First Class. Steglich also qualified for the Infanterie Assault Badge during the French Campaign.

Steglich was promoted to Oberleutnant in October 1941 whilst serving on the Eastern Front, where Fusilier Regiment 27 formed part of 12 Infanterie Division with Armee Gruppe Nord. During his service on the Eastern Front,

Oberleutnant Steglich was awarded the German Cross in Gold on 19 January 1942 in recognition of his gallantry and leadership qualities whilst his unit was part of the German force trapped in the Demjansk pocket. In December 1942, when the officer in command of the unit adjacent to Steglich was killed, Steglich took command and successfully threw back a Soviet breakthrough. For this action he was decorated with the Knight's Cross on 25 January 1943 on the recommendation of his Regimental Commander, Oberst von Mayer. Although the award document dated for 25 January 1943 refers to Steglich as an Oberleutnant, he had in fact been promoted to Hauptmann on 1 January 1943.

After the award of the Knight's Cross, Hauptmann Steglich attended a training course for Battalion Commanders in Antwerp followed by Staff training and Regimental Commander training. He was promoted to Major on 20 April 1944 and in May received the Demjansk Campaign Shield in recognition of his service there in 1942. During May he also received the Close Combat Clasp in Bronze and the Honour Roll Clasp of the German Army.

In November 1944, Major Steglich became Regimental Commander of Grenadier Regiment 1221 on the Western Front. Severely wounded during March 1945, he was awarded the Wound Badge in Silver and was promoted to Oberstleutnant that same month. Martin Steglich became the 816th recipient of the Oakleaves on 5 April 1945 in recognition of his command of Grenadier

Oberst Martin Steglich. This photograph, dating from January 1943, shows Steglich as a Hauptmann. He wears both the Iron Cross Second Class and Eastern Front Campaign Medal ribbons worn from the buttonhole. Steglich later also received the Oakleaves and the Honour Roll Clasp. (Martin Steglich)

Oberstleutnant Steglich showing all his decorations to good effect. Note the Honour Roll Clasp on the Iron Cross ribbon in the buttonhole, and the Bronze Close Combat Clasp over the breast pocket. (Martin Steglich)

Vorläufiges Besitzeugnis

**Der Führer
und Oberste Befehlshaber
der Wehrmacht**
hat

Dem Oberleutnant S t e g l i c h ,
Fhr.I./Füs.Rgt.27

**das Ritterkreuz
des Eisernen Kreuzes**

am ___25.1.1943___ verliehen.

H.Qu.OKH, Den 14.April 1943.

Das Oberkommando des Heers
i. A.

[signature]
Generalmajor

IM NAMEN DES FÜHRERS
UND OBERSTEN BEFEHLSHABERS
DER WEHRMACHT
VERLEIHE ICH
DEM

OBERLEUTNANT
MARTIN STEGLICH
KOMPANIECHEF 5./I. R. 27

**DAS DEUTSCHE KREUZ
IN GOLD**

HAUPTQUARTIER, DEN 15. JANUAR 1942

OBERKOMMANDO DES HEERES

GENERALFELDMARSCHALL

The Preliminary Certificate for Steglich's Knight's Cross. Several months had elapsed between the actions for which the award was given and the issue of the certificate.

The Urkunde for Steglich's Deutsches Kreuz, award for actions during the Demjansk encirclement.

A very rare Commendation Certificate awarded to Leutnant Steglich by the Commander-in-Chief

of the army. This was for actions during the break through of the Stalin Line in 1941.

Hauptquartier O.K.H., den __30.7.1941__

Ich spreche dem

Leutnant S T E G L I C H , Komp.Führer 5./Inf.Regiment 27

meine besondere Anerkennung für seine hervorragenden Leistungen auf dem Schlachtfelde

in bei _____ L A D E L E V A

am _____ 9./10. JULI 1941

aus. *[stamp]* Der Oberbefehlshaber des Heeres

[signature] Brauchitsch

Regiment 1221 during defensive battles against US forces on the Western Front between the Maas and Rhine.

On the cessation of hostilities Oberstleutnant Steglich was taken prisoner by the US Army but was released in August 1945. Oberstleutnant Steglich returned to the service of his country when the German Army was reformed as the *Bundesheer* of the Federal Republic. He was promoted to the rank of Oberst on 1 August 1962. Steglich is a holder of the Verdienstorden of the Federal Republic in both Second and First Classes. He is now retired and holds the position of Chairman with the Ordensgemeinschaft der Ritterkreuzträger.

OBERSTLEUTNANT BRUNO KAHL

Born in Cologne on 23 November 1914, Bruno Kahl commenced his military career in July 1933 after the usual service in the Arbeits-Dienst. Kahl became an officer candidate with a motorised unit in Münster. In April 1935, he was commissioned as a Leutnant and posted to an anti-tank unit in Hannover as a Platoon Commander. In 1936, Leutnant Kahl joined Panzerjäger Abteilung 9 where he became the unit adjutant. He was promoted to Oberleutnant in the summer of 1938 and shortly afterwards assigned to Gebirgs-Panzer-Abwehr-Artillerie Abteilung 48 and with this unit took part in the occupation of Czechoslovakia.

On the outbreak of war in September 1939, Oberleutnant Kahl was serving with the same unit on the southern sector of the front during the Polish Campaign. Kahl also saw action with this unit at Narvik before voluntarily transferring to the Panzer arm in August 1940 and assigned to Panzer Regiment 21.

On 1 June 1941, Kahl was promoted to the rank of Hauptmann and took part in Operation BARBAROSSA with 20 Panzer Division as part of Panzergruppe *Hoth* in the central sector of the Russian Front. On 8 July 1941, he was awarded the Iron Cross Second Class and two days later, the black wound badge for his first wound in action. Just over three months later, Hauptmann Kahl received the Iron Cross First Class and the German Cross in Gold followed in September 1942, all for actions on the Russian Front.

In January 1943, Kahl was promoted to the rank of Major. On 8 February 1943, he was decorated with the Knight's Cross for his success in commanding 3 Kompanie/Panzer Regiment 21 during actions around Toropez in the central sector of the Russian Front. During the summer of that same year, Kahl was posted to the army's *schwere* Panzerjäger Regiment 656 and served with this unit during the Kursk offensive (Operation ZITADELLE). For his successful command of the regiment during this ill-fated offensive, Kahl was decorated with the Oakleaves, as the 270th recipient, on 8 August 1943. Major Kahl then spent some time as the Commander of the Panzerschule at Erlangen before being appointed to command Panzer Regiment *Grossdeutschland* on 1 October 1944.

At the end of hostilities, Kahl, who had been promoted to Oberstleutnant on New Year's Day 1945, went into American captivity and was released in June 1945. He is still alive.

SS-STANDARTENFÜHRER MAX WÜNSCHE

Max Wünsche, one of the best known of Waffen-SS officers, was born in Kittlitz in April 1914, the son of a forester. Wünsche volunteered for the SS in 1934 and attended the Junkerschule at Bad Tölz, being commissioned as an SS-Untersturmführer in 1936. Two years later he was appointed as an ordnance officer, then as an adjutant on Hitler's staff. He served on Hitler's staff during the Polish Campaign and thereafter returned to a combat posting with the *Leibstandarte* in time to take part in the battles in France with the Kradschützenkompanie, winning both Second and First Class Iron Crosses.

Wünsche also saw service during the Greek and Jugoslavian campaigns before being given command of the Sturmgeschutz Abteilung of the *Leibstandarte* in time for the invasion of the Soviet Union. Subsequently, he also commanded the 1 Abteilung of the division's Panzer Regiment. Wünsche's personal gallantry was recognised by the award of the Knight's Cross on 28 February 1943 for service during the intense fighting during the battle for Kharkov. After the conclusion of the battle, Wünsche was promoted to SS-Obersturmbannführer and transferred to take command of the newly formed Panzer Regiment 12 in the 12 SS Panzer Division *Hitlerjugend*.

The ferocious defence of the area around Caen and Falaise by the young soldiers of the *Hitlerjugend* Division is legendary and the gallantry and leadership of Wünsche played no small part in keeping up the high degree of morale and fighting spirit of these troops. During the fighting which raged around Hill 112, *Hitlerjugend* was responsible for the destruction of over 250 enemy tanks. For the stubborn defence of his divisional area, as well as for his own personal bravery, Max Wünsche was decorated with the Oakleaves on 11 August 1944 and was promoted to the rank of SS-Standartenführer. Wünsche was captured on 24 August 1944, after a rearguard action around the Falaise Gap assisting the escape of part of VII Armee. At the time of his capture, he had been recommended for the Swords.

Wünsche's military career had been extremely successful. As a young man of only 30, he had reached the rank of full Colonel, was commanding a Panzer Regiment, and had been decorated with the coveted Oakleaves. Max Wünsche was held in British captivity until 1948. He is still alive.

SS-STANDARTENFÜHRER ALBERT FREY

The son of a baker, Albert Frey was born in Heidelberg on 16 February 1913. Joining the SS in 1933, Frey served in the *Deutschland* Standarte and was selected for officer training at the SS Junkerschule Braunschweig in 1937. He was commissioned as an SS-Untersturmführer in the spring of 1938 and was posted to the élite *Leibstandarte SS Adolf Hitler*.

During the Polish campaign Frey, by now an SS-Obersturmführer, was decorated with the Iron Cross Second Class. This was followed by the First Class during the French Campaign in the following June.

Oberstleutnant Bruno Kahl. The cloth embroidered version of the German Cross in Gold is visible just below the breast eagle. Wear of what appears to be a white shirt with the black panzer jacket (Panzerjacke) was fairly uncommon. It is interesting to note that Kahl is wearing a General Assault rather than a Panzer Assault Badge next to his Iron Cross. (Bruno Kahl)

Below left: In this photograph, SS-Standartenführer Max Wünsche wears the SS version of the special black Panzerjacke. It has smaller lapels and has the front cut vertically rather than at an angle. At the time the photograph was taken, Wünsche held the rank of Sturmbannführer. (Munin Verlag)

Below right: SS-Standartenführer Albert Frey. The photograph shows Frey as an Obersturmbannführer commanding SS Panzer Grenadier Regiment 1. Frey became the 359th recipient of the Oakleaves on 27 December 1943 whilst on the Eastern Front. (Arthur Charlton)

After the conclusion of the battle for France, the *Leibstandarte* served in the Greek and Jugoslavian Campaigns prior to the commencement of Operation BARBAROSSA. Frey had by then reached the rank of SS-Hauptsturmführer and was beginning to make a name for himself as a cool, calm and calculating officer and a good example to his men. During the fighting around Taganrog, Frey distinguished himself in the destruction by his battalion of two Soviet armoured trains which had been causing heavy losses. For his part in this action, he was decorated with the German Cross in Gold, on 17 November 1941.

During the upgrading of the *Leibstandarte* to the status of a Panzer Division, Albert Frey was promoted to the rank of SS-Sturmbannführer, commanding 1 Bataillon of the Panzer Grenadier Regiment. 1943 saw the *Leibstandarte* involved in the heavy fighting around Kharkov. Frey's unit acquitted itself well during the weeks of savage fighting that ensued and, in honour of his own personal gallantry and his leadership of the Battalion and also to honour the unit itself and its many fallen, Frey was decorated with the Knight's Cross on 17 November 1941.

Frey was further promoted in March 1943, to SS-Obersturmbannführer commanding the Panzer Grenadier Regiment, and saw action during the Battle of Kursk. This was followed by a spell in Italy before returning to the Eastern Front in December 1943. The regiment was heavily involved in the fierce fighting around Kiev and, on several occasions, Frey's men were successful in holding back Soviet attacks despite heavy artillery bombardment. Heavily reinforced Soviet units with tank support tried desperately to break through the German defences and, in recognition of the prime role played by his regiment in denying the Soviet's success and also in recognition of his own personal courage, Frey was decorated with the Oakleaves on 20 December 1943.

Frey continued to serve with the regiment in Normandy, the Ardennes and Hungary. He spent some time in American captivity at the end of the war before being released to return to his home. He is still alive.

SS-STANDARTENFÜHRER JOACHIM PEIPER

Joachim or 'Jochen' Peiper has become one of the best known of all Waffen-SS soldiers. To some, he represented the best features of the Waffen-SS. His typical Nordic good looks, his fearless bravery and his unceasing loyalty all served to endear him to his men. On the other hand, the notoriety which Kampfgruppe 'Peiper' attracted during the Ardennes Offensive and Peiper's subsequent castigation in the media led to him being branded as a callous war criminal and, ultimately, to his murder 31 years after the war's end.

Peiper was born on 30 January 1915 in Berlin, the son of an army officer. He volunteered for the SS in 1934 and was accepted into the SS Reitersturmbann. After attending the SS Junkerschule Braunschweig, he was commissioned as an SS-Untersturmführer in 1936 and posted to the élite *Leibstandarte*. From

SS-Standartenführer Jochen Peiper. Shown here as a Sturmbannführer, Peiper wears the old-style field cap but with the standard type metal cap insignia. Just visible on his shoulder straps are the 'LAH' gilt metal divisional monograms. (Völkischer Beobachter)

A more formal portrait shot of Peiper, taken just after the award of his Knight's Cross in March 1943. Peiper was also often photographed wearing the smart black Panzer uniform. (Völkischer Beobachter)

1938 until the start of the war, he served as an adjutant on Heinrich Himmler's staff.

When war broke out, he served in the Polish Campaign as an SS-Hauptsturmführer and commander of II Kompanie of the *Leibstandarte*. During the campaign in the West, he was awarded the Iron Cross Second Class and First Class within two months.

By 1941, Hauptsturmführer Peiper was serving with the *Leibstandarte* on the Eastern Front with III Bataillon. In 1943, the *Leibstandarte* was involved in the recapture of Kharkov. Peiper, by now a Sturmbannführer commanding III Bataillon was given the task of taking an armoured infantry column behind the enemy lines to make contact with the isolated 320 Infantry Division under General Postel and to evacuate them to safety. Peiper accomplished this task with consummate skill, rescuing his army comrades and their wounded and escorting them the 25 kilometres through to the River Donez where the divisional convoy crossed over the frozen ice. Peiper's armoured infantry vehicles were too heavy to cross over and Peiper had to fight his way back, establishing a bridgehead over the Donez at Federowka and destroying three Soviet tanks on the way. For his achievement, he was recommended for the Knight's Cross by 'Sepp' Dietrich on 8 March. The award was approved by Hitler on 9 March. Peiper was also awarded the German Cross on 6 May 1943.

In November 1943, Peiper was given command of the *Leibstandarte*'s Panzer Regiment. At the end of that year, Peiper's Panzer Regiment took part in an attack with an armoured battle group east of Zhitomir, breaking through the enemy lines. Operating up to 30 kilometres inside enemy territory, Peiper's Panzers threw the Soviets into disarray as they charged around dispensing death and destruction. His unit destroyed over 100 Soviet tanks, 76 anti-tank weapons, 22 artillery pieces and much other equipment. Peiper received a telegram from Hitler.

In thankful appreciation of your heroic actions in the battle for the future of our people, I award you, as the 377th soldier of the armed forces, the Oakleaves to the Knight's Cross of the Iron Cross. Adolf Hitler.

On the Western Front following the Allied invasion of Normandy, Peiper's Panzer regiment destroyed over 100 enemy tanks during the fierce defensive battles. For the last great offensive in the west, through the Ardennes, Peiper commanded the armoured battle group of the *Leibstandarte*. Initially a great success, Peiper and his massive King Tiger tanks thundered through the American lines. However, lack of fuel, Allied air superiority and poor logistic support led to the inevitable foundering of the offensive. Kampfgruppe 'Peiper' was eventually forced to abandon its tanks but eventually reached safety in the German lines.

It was not, however, the skill and bravery in action of the Kampfgruppe which was to bring Peiper fame during this particular battle. Instead, that was overshadowed: the battle brought him notoriety. On 16 December, a number of US PoW's had been assembled at the Malmedy crossroads. A passing German unit opened fire on them, killing 74. This massacre was to be Peiper's undoing after the war. In the meantime, however, unaware of this event, Peiper was decorated with the Swords on 28 December 1944 and promoted to Standartenführer in recognition of his unit's achievements during the Ardennes offensive.

When he surrendered in 1945, Peiper was held for trial for his alleged responsibility for the Malmedy massacre. The trial was held at Dachau. Peiper had already fully accepted that he should be held responsible for any actions committed by men under his command but denied allegations that any order for the execution of prisoners was given. Indeed, it was never established that such orders had been given. Peiper was sentenced to death by his 'court' but the outcry which followed the inquiry into the interrogation techniques forced a commutation of his sentence to life imprisonment, from which he was released in 1956.

The trials themselves were a travesty of justice and eventually became the result of an enquiry. It was established that investigating interrogators had used both physical and psychological torture, including rigging fake executions to extract confession. It was unrealistic to expect an objective trial for a senior SS officer after the war. Certainly, the circumstantial evidence produced and the methods used in interrogation of prisoners would never have allowed a conviction in today's courts.

The stain these events left on his character was to follow him through his civilian life. Eventually, with the full knowledge of the French authorities, he settled in Traves but was discovered by left wing terrorists and brutally murdered in 1976. Needless to say, his killers have never been apprehended.

Whatever the allegations which were brought against him, there can be no doubting Peiper's personal qualities as a brave and resourceful soldier, well-liked and respected by his superiors and held in great affection by his men. He was a worthy winner of Germany's highest gallantry awards.

SS-HAUPTSTURMFÜHRER HEINZ MACHER

A Saxon, born in Chemnitz in December 1919, Heinz Macher enlisted into the SS in April 1939 after completing his compulsory Reichsarbeitsdienst service. He joined 2 Kompanie/SS Pionierebataillon in Dresden and saw much active service in the Polish, Western and Balkan campaigns before attending an Officer Training Course and being commissioned in 1942. He then joined 16 (Pioniere) Kompanie/SS Standarte *Deutschland*.

In early March 1943, an armoured unit of the *Das Reich* Division reached the outskirts of Kharkov only to find their way blocked by an anti-tank ditch 200 metres from the first houses, in which Soviet defenders were established in force. On the night of 11/12 March, Heinz Macher and an assault group from his Pioniere Kompanie launched an attack under cover of darkness. In furious hand to hand fighting, Macher and his men established a bridgehead 300 metres deep into the Soviet lines and held their position until armour from the Panzer group could cross.

Macher's attack was a total success. No German lives were lost, and only six

Heinz Macher with men of his Pioniere Kompanie on the Eastern Front in 1943. He wears no rank insignia whatsoever on his short double-breasted camouflage jacket. This style of jacket is based on the black Panzerjacke. Officers silver piping is worn on his field cap, however, as is the black inverted 'V' soutache of engineer troops. (Heinz Macher)

men wounded. Enemy losses were 28 taken prisoner and 90 killed. A large number of small arms, twelve mortars, five anti-tank guns and four field guns were captured. The advance of the *Das Reich* assault group was possible solely due to the bravery and skill of Macher and his men. On 3 April 1943 Macher was decorated with the Knight's Cross in recognition of his achievement.

During the Normandy battles, Macher and his men threw back numerous Allied attacks on their positions. Over a period of just eight days, 37 attacks were rebuffed and Macher's men launched 29 counter-attacks. On 19 August 1944, Macher became the 554th recipient of the Oakleaves for his service in Normandy. In January 1945, Macher saw action in the defence of Kustrin before successfully making his way west where he surrendered to the Anglo-American forces at the end of the war. Macher is still alive.

OBERST HEINZ VON BRESE

Heinz von Brese was born in Dresden in 1914. Volunteering for military service at the age of 20, he was commissioned in 1936 as an Infantry Leutnant. On the outbreak of war Heinz von Brese was serving with the rank of Oberleutnant and was Battalion Adjutant to 2/Infanterie Regiment 10. With this unit, he saw action in the Polish Campaign, winning the Iron Cross Second Class. The Iron Cross First Class followed during the French Campaign where von Brese served as a Company Commander.

By 1942, von Brese had reached the rank of Hauptmann and held the German Cross in Gold. He was given command of a Battle Group on the Eastern Front in December 1942, and was serving with it when the battle of Stalingrad was reaching its peak in May 1943. Both von Brese, and his predecessor as Battle Group commander, Major Sauerbruch, were responsible for the defence of a bridge over the river Don which had been constructed for the resupply of the beleaguered German forces against overwhelming Soviet odds. The German troops defending the bridge were a mixed bunch, including all sorts of stragglers, at one point reaching divisional strength. Command of such a large body of men was a considerable responsibility for a young captain. For his successful defence of this important bridge, von Brese was decorated with the Knight's Cross on 15 May 1943 and promoted to the rank of Major. Sauerbruch also received the Knight's Cross.

In 1944, Heinz von Brese was serving in the Tscherkassy pocket with 14 Panzer Division. He had by then reached the rank of Oberstleutnant. For actions during this period, he became the 441st recipient of the Oakleaves on 6 April 1944.

Heinz von Brese was subsequently posted to a Panzertruppe Training School and then attended a course for Divisional Commanders before being given command of the elite Panzer Fusilier Regiment *Grossdeutschland* with the rank of Oberst in September 1944.

At the conclusion of hostilities, von Brese and his men went into Soviet captivity. Heinz von Brese survived the war and now lives in retirement in Freiburg.

A formal portrait study of Macher as a Hauptsturmführer after the award of the Oakleaves in 1944. Just visible on the left cuff is the Deutschland regimental cuffband, whilst on the right arm can be seen the award badge for single-handed destruction of an enemy tank. (Heinz Macher)

At an award ceremony at the Reichskanzlei in 1944, von Brese has just received the Oakleaves personally from Hitler. (Heinz von Brese)

Oberstleutnant von Brese on the Eastern Front, wearing the M43 general issue field cap and what appears to be the rubberised waterproof greatcoat of the type used by motor cyclists, and carrying powerful field glasses around his neck. (Heinz von Brese)

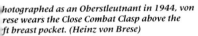

Photographed as an Oberstleutnant in 1944, von Brese wears the Close Combat Clasp above the left breast pocket. (Heinz von Brese)

SS-OBERSTURMBANNFÜHRER MARTIN GROSS

Martin Gross was the son of a railway official and was born on 15 April 1911 in Frankfurt. He joined the SS in May 1933, volunteering for the *Leibstandarte* in Berlin. He was commissioned as an SS-Untersturmführer in 1935 and promoted to the rank of SS-Obersturmführer in 1937. He saw action in the occupation of Austria and the Sudetenland. During the Polish Campaign Obersturmführer Gross served as a platoon commander with 1 Kompanie of the *Leibstandarte*, winning the Iron Cross Second Class. In 1940, he was promoted to SS-Hauptsturmführer commanding the same Kompanie and was awarded the Iron Cross First Class during the campaign in the West.

On the Eastern Front in 1941, Gross commanded 5 Kompanie at Rostov where he was seriously wounded. After his recovery he was posted to a staff job for a time before returning to command II/Panzer Regiment of the *Leibstandarte* and was promoted to SS-Sturmbannführer in January 1943. During the battle for Kharkov in March 1943, Gross was decorated with the German Cross in Gold.

The morning of 12 July 1943 found Gross with his Abteilung in the area around Bjelgorod, when the Soviet forces launched an attack on his position. Despite the seriousness of his situation and the Soviet superiority in numbers, Gross not only managed to throw back the attackers but actually encircled and

A smiling Sturmbannführer Martin Gross photographed on the Eastern Front in 1943. Gross wears the SS version of the field grey assault gun tunic and just visible on the shoulder straps, the numeral '1'. Gross served in SS Panzer Regiment 1. (Martin Gross)

SS-Obersturmbannführer Günther-Eberhard Wisliceny. Open-necked tunics such as the one worn by Wisliceny in this photograph are rather uncommon. He wears the Hitler Jugend golden badge of honour just above the Iron Cross First Class. (Günther-Eberhard Wisliceny)

destroyed them. In three hours of intense combat, Gross was responsible for the destruction of 90 enemy tanks and the plucky *Leibstandarte* grenadiers destroyed a further 30 in close quarter fighting. The battlefield was a literal graveyard of Soviet armour. For his amazing achievement, Gross was decorated with the Knight's Cross on 22 July 1943. Gross insisted that he wore the decoration as much in recognition of his brave comrades as for his own gallantry.

By the summer of 1944, the *Leibstandarte* had been transferred to the Western Front and was thrown into the attempt to stem the Allied advance into Normandy. Gross, however, was to remain on the Eastern Front where he was given command of a Panzer Brigade, and he saw continuous action around Riga and Lithuania.

In November 1944, Gross was promoted to SS-Obersturmbannführer and was given command of Panzer Regiment 12 in the now battle-tested 12 SS Panzer Division *Hitlerjugend*, and they saw action in the Ardennes Offensive and subsequently in Hungary. Gross was with the division when it surrendered to US forces in Austria in May 1945. The division consisted of a mere 455 men and one solitary tank.

Martin Gross lived in retirement in Luer until his death in 1985.

SS-OBERSTURMBANNFÜHRER GÜNTHER-EBERHARD WISLICENY

Wisliceny was born on 5 September 1912, the son of an East-Prussian estate owner. In March 1933 Wisliceny joined the SS in Berlin, being commissioned into the elite *Leibstandarte SS Adolf Hitler* as an SS-Untersturmführer in March 1935. By 1938, he was serving as a Platoon Commander in 8 Kompanie of the *Der Führer* Regiment, with the rank of SS-Obersturmführer.

Wisliceny was awarded the Iron Cross Second Class in July 1941, during the opening moves of Operation BARBAROSSA. This was followed by the First Class in November of the same year during the drive on Moscow. Shortly afterwards, Wisliceny was severely wounded and spent several months hospitalised before returning to duty in March 1942 as Company Commander of 8 Kompanie/SS Regiment *Der Führer*.

The SS Division *Das Reich* of which *Der Führer* was a part was being refitted and reformed during spring 1942. During this reformation, Wisliceny was given command of 3 Bataillon/Panzer Grenadier Regiment *Deutschland* and was further rewarded in April 1943 with the German Cross in Gold and promotion to the rank of SS-Sturmbannführer.

At the beginning of July 1943, the German forces were concentrating for an operation which Hitler hoped would strike a decisive blow at the Soviet forces around Kursk and flatten out the large 'bulge' of Soviet-held territory. Wisliceny's battalion served at the forefront of the SS-Panzerkorps as the German attack started. Despite the heaviest defensive fire, Wisliceny and his men stormed forward regardless. Wisliceny himself was wounded for the third time during the assault but remained at the head of his men. His battalion was the only one to break completely through the Soviet defences and for this achievement he was awarded the Knight's Cross on 30 July 1943.

In April of the following year, Wisliceny was in command of Panzer Grenadier Regiment *Deutschland*, refitting in the south of France. By this time he held the rank of SS-Obersturmbannführer. With the Allied invasion of Normandy in June 1944, it was not to be long before the *Deutschland* Regiment along with the rest of the *Das Reich* Division, was thrown into the furious fighting with the Anglo-American invaders. Initially committed to the battle piecemeal, it was not until 10 July that *Das Reich* fought as a unified division, by which time it had already suffered a high casualty rate. It was still, however, a formidable fighting force and Wisliceny's regiment fought doggedly through-out the Normandy battles and through the Falaise Gap, eventually retreating over the Seine at Elbeuf.

Deutschland subsequently fought in Hungary, where *Das Reich* was sent to bolster the German forces against the Soviet onslaught. In recognition of his participation in the furious hand to hand combat which took place, Wisliceny was decorated with the Close Combat Clasp in Gold, and, when wounded in action again shortly afterwards, the Wound Badge in Gold. On 26 December 1944, Wisliceny was awarded the Oakleaves to his Knight's Cross for actions against the US forces during the Normandy Campaign.

Wisliceny saw further action in the Ardennes Offensive and the defence of Vienna. On 6 May 1945, he was awarded the Swords, presented to him by the Commander of the 6 SS Panzerarmee, Josef 'Sepp' Dietrich. Two days later Wisliceny marched at the head of his men, into American captivity and was thereafter handed over to the French, who held him until 1951.

Günther-Eberhard Wisliceny retired to Hannover where he lived until his death in 1985.

OBERLEUTNANT GERHARD KONOPKA

Born on 27 March 1911, Gerhard Konopka was a senior ranking officer in the Reichsarbeitsdienst, holding the rank of Arbeitsführer. He served with Grenadier Regiment *Grossdeutschland*, winning the German Cross in Gold during the defensive actions around Rzhev. The regiment took a severe pounding during these battles and was withdrawn from the line to be refitted and at the same time was expanded and upgraded to a Panzer Grenadier Division.

In August 1943, the Panzer-grenadier regiment of the division was involved in heavy action following the major Soviet offensive after the end of the unsuccessful German attack on the Kursk salient. On 3 August 1943, the 2 Bataillon of the regiment attacked Soviet positions near Alissowa. Though strongly defended, the Soviet positions on the hill known as 'Yellow Hill' were over-run by Konopka and his men in hard fought combat involving fierce hand to hand fighting. The capture of this hill gave the regiment an important vantage point overlooking enemy-held territory. For this achievement, Gerhard Konopka was decorated with the Knight's Cross on 29 August 1943.

Photographed on the Eastern Front Oberleutnant Gerhard Konopka wears four of the special badges for single-handed destruction of an enemy tank. The 'GD' monogram of the **Grossdeutschland** Division can just be seen on the shoulder straps. (Gerhard Konopka)

Hauptmann Hans Lex, Company Commander with 7 Kompanie, Panzer Regiment **Grossdeutschland**. He wears the silver Panzer Assault Badge on his left breast pocket and the small gilt 'GD' monograms can just be discerned on the shoulder straps. (Hans Lex)

Konopka's personal daring is further attested to by the fact that he was four times decorated with the Badge for single-handed destruction of a tank. Hauptmann Konopka survived the war and lives today in retirement.

HAUPTMANN HANS LEX

Born on 21 January 1916, Hans Lex served with 7 Kompanie, Panzer Regiment *Grossdeutschland*. In July 1943, *Grossdeutschland* was heavily involved in the battle for the Kursk salient, Operation ZITADELLE. During the last few days of the offensive, east of Werchopenje, Lex, with a single tank, destroyed 16 enemy T34's and through his quick thinking and resolve, averted a strong enemy threat to the regiment's flank. For this achievement, Hauptmann Lex was awarded the Knight's Cross on 17 September 1943. In a special Regimental Order of the Day on 27 September, the Regimental Commander praised Lex, saying:

The Regiment is proud of its bearer of this high award. Hauptmann Lex will be a great example for his men in future.

HAUPTMANN RUDOLF SIGMUND

Rudolf Sigmund was born in Hardheim in March 1915. Very little is known about his early career, but he joined the *Luftwaffe* in 1936 and initially served in day fighters, shooting down two enemy aircraft before transferring to night fighting duties.

Luftwaffe *night fighter ace Hauptmann Rudolf Sigmund, wearing the Night Fighter Clasp worn above the left breast pocket. Sigmund was accidentally shot down by his own flak. (Author Collection)*

Below left: Oberst Karl-Heinz Schulz-Lepel photographed in Courland in November 1944, showing a fine array of awards, including the cloth version of the German Cross in Gold, the Honour Roll Clasp on the buttonhole ribbon; the Wound Badge being worn is of the so called 'Spanish' pattern. (Karl-Heinz Schulz-Lepel)

Below right: This fine postwar photograph of Schulz-Lepel in the uniform of the West German **Bundeswehr** *allows clear comparison of the wartime and postwar versions of all of his decorations. The swastika has been deleted from them all. (Karl-Heinz Schulz-Lepel)*

Sigmund flew Bf 110 fighter bombers. These aircraft suffered badly at the hands of the Spitfire and Hurricane fighters of the RAF and were transferred to night operations, in which they were a great success. Sigmund became Staffel-kapitän with 11 Staffel of IV/Nachtjagdgeschwader 1, flying from Leeuwarden in Holland, during the spring of 1942. Sigmund became a skilled night-fighter pilot. During one sortie in June 1943 he succeeded in downing three British bombers within just 14 minutes plus a fourth just one hour later.

Sigmund's Knight's Cross winning action came on the night of 25/26 July 1943. Halifax bombers from No 158 Squadron, RAF, based at RAF Lisset in Yorkshire were intercepted by aircraft of NJG1 over Holland. In one Halifax, rear gunner Sergeant Jock Loudoun spotted a Bf 110 coming from behind and below at a very acute angle. He managed to get off a burst with his four 0.303in Browning machine-guns before his own aircraft was badly hit, immediately catching fire. As the stricken aircraft plummeted from the sky, only Sergeant Loudoun managed to bale out. The rest of the crew are presumed to have been killed. Although injured, Loudoun landed safely but was betrayed to the Germans and spent the rest of the war in Prisoner of War Stalag IVB in eastern Germany.

What Jock Loudoun did not know at the time was that his brief burst of fire had struck home. Sigmund and his radio operator/air gunner were both wounded and his port engine was aflame. When he realised that his comrade was also wounded, Sigmund decided to stay with the aircraft and attempt to make it back to his base. Despite being half blinded by blood from a head wound, he succeeded in landing his still burning aircraft. When he was treated in hospital for his wounds, several pieces of shrapnel were removed from his shoulder and forehead.

For shooting down the enemy aircraft and returning his damaged aircraft to base despite severe wounds, Sigmund was awarded the Knight's Cross on 2 August 1943. The day before, 1 August, Sigmund had been transferred to take over command of III/NJG3, and the official award ceremony for his Knight's Cross was carried out on 16 August 1943 at Stade, near Hamburg where NJG3 was based. The award was made by General der Nachtjäger Josef Kammhuber.

On 31 October 1943, after carrying out an attack on enemy bombers over Munich, Sigmund's Bf 110 was hit by friendly anti-aircraft units as he returned to Stade. Sigmund's final score at his date of death was 28 enemy aircraft, making him one of the top night fighter aces.

OBERSTLEUTNANT KARL-HEINZ SCHULZ-LEPEL

Karl-Heinz Schulz-Lepel served during World War Two with Infanterie Regiment 557, part of 329 Infanterie Division, known as the 'Hammer' Division after the divisional badge. This division spent its whole life on the Eastern Front.

The division served with Armeegruppe Nord and was heavily involved in the battles to relieve the encircled German units in the Demjansk pocket. For his part in these fierce battles, Karl-Heinz Schulz-Lepel was awarded the German Cross in Gold on 12 November 1942. This was followed by the Knight's Cross in September of 1943 whilst still serving on the same sector of the front, for gallantry in the face of the enemy. The regiment was involved in the fighting withdrawal through Courland where it was still located at the end of the war.

Karl-Heinz Schulz-Lepel survived the war and went on to serve in the West German Bundesheer after his release from Soviet captivity. He reached the rank of Oberstleutnant before retiring.

Herr Schulz-Lepel is still alive and lives in retirement.

STABSFELDWEBEL HEINRICH GATH

A highly competent and experienced combat NCO, Heinrich Gath was a Troop Commander with Panzer Aufklärungsabteilung 2, which formed part of 2 Panzer Division. One of Germany's first Panzer divisions, it had served all through the occupation of Austria, the invasion of Poland, the Western Campaign, the Greek and Jugoslavian Campaigns and the invasion of the Soviet Union. Heinrich Gath received the Knight's Cross on 11 October 1943 for actions during combat on the Dnieper Line in the southern sector of the Eastern Front.

During 1944, 2 Panzer division saw action in the Normandy battles where it was progressively reduced in strength through severe fighting until, when withdrawn through the Falaise Gap in August, the once mighty Panzer division had a strength of only 25 tanks. Refitted, the division took part in the Ardennes Offensive where it again suffered heavy losses. By 1945, it had a strength of just four tanks and 200 men. The division surrendered at Fulda in April 1945.

OBERFELDWEBEL WALTER WRIEDT

Oberfeldwebel Walter Wriedt served with 13 Kompanie/Gebirgsjäger Regiment 138, part of 3 Gebirgs Division. The division was originally formed from the 5th and 7th Divisions of the Austrian Army, gained by Germany after the *Anschluss* in 1938.

The regiment served in the Polish Campaign, in the invasion of Norway under General Dietl and thence into Finland from where it struck into the Soviet Union during Operation BARBAROSSA. Wriedt's unit operated on the Murmansk Front, patrolling and engaging the enemy in skirmishing actions for over a year before being attached to Heeresgruppe Nord in August 1942.

This attachment was short lived and the division was soon rushed south as the situation on that part of the front deteriorated with threatened Soviet offensives. Wriedt was decorated with the German Cross in Gold on 18 January 1943.

The regiment suffered heavy casualties on the southern sector of the Eastern Front in late 1943 as the Rumanians attacked from the West and the Soviets

Stabsfeldwebel Heinrich Gath. In this clear shot can be seen the Knight's Cross, the Close Combat Clasp, Iron Cross First Class, Panzer Assault Badge and Wound Badge. Stabsfeldwebel rank is indicated by three pips on the braid edged shoulder strap. (Heinrich Gath)

In this photograph, Oberfeldwebel Walter Wriedt wears the Bergmütze cap of the mountain troops, complete with Edelweiss emblem. Unusually, no Iron Cross Second Class ribbon is being worn, either in the buttonhole or ribbon bar. (Brian L Davis)

from the East. During this bitter fighting, on 25 October 1943, Oberfeldwebel Wriedt was decorated with the Knight's Cross of the Iron Cross for his personal courage in action.

Wriedt's division spent the remainder of the war on the Eastern Front, surrendering to the Red Army in Upper Silesia in May 1945.

SS-UNTERSTURMFÜHRER ALFRED SIEGLING

Alfred Siegling was born on 15 March 1918 in Erlau and joined the SS in 1938, entering 16 Kompanie, SS-Standarte *Deutschland* in Ellwangen. He served with the *Deutschland* Regiment in the Polish Campaign, being promoted to SS-Sturmann on 1 November 1939. Later, during the advance into France, Siegling was decorated with the Iron Cross Second Class.

During the invasion of the Soviet Union, Siegling, by then an SS-Unterscharführer, was serving with 1 Kompanie, SS Panzer Aufklärungsabteilung 2, part of the SS *Reich* Division (later to become 2 SS Panzer Division *Das Reich*). On 21 July 1942, Siegling was awarded the Panzer Assault Badge in Bronze and, in April 1943, he was awarded the Iron Cross First Class in recognition of actions in the fierce fighting around Kharkov.

Alfred Siegling was decorated with the Knight's Cross on 2 December 1943 in recognition of a particularly successful reconnaissance mission he had undertaken. He had been ordered to carry out a survey of the area around a small village where Soviet movement was suspected. Travelling at high speed in their Bussing-Nag eight-wheel armoured cars, Siegling's patrol reached the village, surrounded by swampy marshland. Siegling immediately spotted numbers of Soviet armoured vehicles parked amongst the houses. Given the terrain, to turn and retreat would have been impossible, so Siegling gave the order to 'put the foot down' and his two armoured cars sped through the village flat out and were gone before the startled Soviets could react.

Whilst en route back to his own lines, the patrol met a long Soviet armoured column. Once again Siegling decided to attempt to bluff his way through rather than retreat, and drove straight along the length of the enemy column impatiently waving the Russians aside. The enemy, presumably either not recognising the German vehicles or thinking them to be captured vehicles crewed by Russians, let Siegling's patrol pass by without a shot being fired.

All this time Siegling's radio operators were relaying information about these Soviet movements back to their own headquarters. On his return, Siegling found that his information had been invaluable. Forewarned of the impending Soviet attack, the Germans were ready for them and the attempted

SS-Untersturmführer Alfred Siegling, photographed when he held the rank of Oberscharführer. Visible just above the pip on the shoulder strap is a small white metal letter 'A' for Aufklärungstruppe. (Alfred Siegling)

In this photograph, Major Josef Rettemeier wears the 'Afrika' campaign cuff title on the left sleeve of his black Panzerjacke. He also wears the officers pattern M38 field cap, generally superseded by the M43 type cap by the time this photograph was taken in 1944. (Josef Rettemeier)

Soviet breakthrough failed with heavy losses. This was entirely due to the information gathered by Siegling's patrol and to his cool headed and daring bluff.

On 1 November 1944, Siegling was commissioned as an SS-Untersturm-führer. He served with the Panzer Aufklärungsabteilung throughout the remainder of the war, seeing action on both Eastern and Western Fronts before surrendering with the rest of the division to US forces in May 1945. Alfred Siegling died on 5 September 1984.

MAJOR JOSEF RETTEMEIER

Born on 17 September 1914 in Niederdollendorf, near Bonn, Josef Rettemeier commenced his military career with 6 (Prussian) Kraftfahrabteilung in Munster. After attending military academy in Dresden, he was commissioned as a Leutnant in 1936 and served with Panzerabwehrabteilung 22 as a Platoon Commander. Subsequently, he served with Panzerabwehrabteilung 30 as a Company Commander and with Panzerabwehrabteilung 46 in Vienna as Battalion Adjutant. By the outbreak of war in 1939, he was serving as an Adjutant with Schutzen Regiment 82.

Rettemeier later served with 9 Panzer Division during the French Campaign, where the division was part of Panzergruppe *Guderian*, followed by service with an anti-tank unit, Panzerjägerabteilung 111, part of 111 Infanterie Division.

By 1942, Rettemeier was a Company Commander with Panzer Regiment 5, part of 5 Leichte Division in North Africa. During the division's service in Africa, it was reformed as 21 Panzer Division. In 1943, Rettemeier was transferred from Africa to the Eastern Front.

The 5 Panzerabteilung in which Rettemeier served was located in the central sector of the Eastern Front where, for his command of the unit during combat around Witebsk and Rogatschew along the road to Smolensk, he was awarded the Knight's Cross on 5 December 1943. Just over three months later, on 13 March 1944, he became the 425th recipient of the Oakleaves for his success in command of the unit on the Eastern Front.

Rettemeier was a fine example of a gallant soldier and a fine leader of men. He was shortly in the thick of the action again, with the renowned *Panzer Lehr* Division during the defensive battles in Normandy. Despite its formidable power, *Panzer Lehr* was no match for the overwhelming Allied *matériel* superiority, particularly in the air, and large numbers of its tanks fell victim to Allied fighter bombers. The division was virtually annihilated by July 1944.

Rettemeier was subsequently posted to the Officer Cadet School at Erlangen. There he remained until the end of the war.

When the German army was reformed in 1956, Rettemeier rejoined the armed forces and served at the Bundeswehr's Panzertruppeschule at Munster. He became deputy Divisional Commander of 3 Panzer Division, retiring in 1972. His military career was not yet over, however, and he went on to become a military adviser to the Nationalist Chinese forces on Taiwan for three years. Rettemeier reached the rank of Oberst before retiring from military life.

1944
THE SHRINKING REICH

By 1 January 1944, the advancing Soviet forces were only 43 kilometres from the Polish border and crossed it just three days later. Kirovograd in the Ukraine was captured by the advancing Red Army on 8 January and Novgorod was liberated on 19 January.

April found the Red Army entering Rumania, whilst the offensive in the Ukraine succeeded in recapturing Odessa. Soon the Soviets had taken Sebastopol and on 13 May, the entire Crimea was once again in Russian hands. In June, the Red Army launched a major offensive into Byelorussia and by the following month Vilna in Lithuania had fallen and the Russians had reached the outskirts of Warsaw.

In August 1943, the Polish Home Army began its uprising in Warsaw hoping for Soviet intervention and the supply of arms and food. August was a momentous month for the Third Reich when Soviet gunfire fell on German soil for the first time, on the occasion of the artillery bombardment of Mariampole in East Prussia. The end of August found the Red Army occupying Bucharest. Two days afterwards, they reached Bulgaria.

In October, the Germans finally crushed the Polish Home Army in Warsaw and had a further success on the Eastern Front when three Russian Corps were surrounded and destroyed at Debrecen during a local German counter-attack. Such a local success could hardly alter the final outcome on the rapidly crumbling Eastern Front and by the end of the month, Army Group North was cut off in Courland. It remained isolated there until the end of the war.

On the Italian Front, the year had started with the Allies advancing slowly but steadily. In an attempt to outflank the German defenders, Allied troops were landed by sea at Anzio and Nettuno on 22 January. Although the Germans attacked fiercely, they could not dislodge the Allied bridgehead but the Allies did suffer heavy losses. By mid-February, the Allies were being held at Monte Cassino. The subsequent Allied bombing raid on the abbey merely created a superb defensive position to be occupied by the Germans. The German counter-attack on Anzio had begun to falter but was renewed again towards the end of February.

On 11 May, the Allied forces in Italy began their attack on the Gustav line and, four days later, after an abortive counter-attack, the German defenders were forced to withdraw. On 18 May, the Germans also withdrew from Cassino. Although over ten thousand of the German defenders had died at Cassino, the Allies lost over forty thousand in dislodging them.

The beginning of June saw the Allies making good headway in Italy and, on the 4th, Rome was occupied by the Fifth Army.

All of these events were to seem insignificant, however, when the long awaited invasion of Europe commenced on the Normandy coast on 6 June. At first, the German High Command were hesitant, thinking that it might be

Fellow 'aces' and good friends, 'Ajax' Bleichrodt, left, and Erich Topp, centre, aboard a U-boat in   *1944. (Jak P. Mallmann Showell/Dr Wolf Heinrich Bleichrodt)*

diversion and that a second invasion force would land elsewhere. Vital reserves were thus held from the battlefield until too late. Within six days, the Allies had landed over three hundred and twenty thousand troops and all of the four beachheads had linked up. On 29 June, the Americans liberated Cherbourg.

By the beginning of July, almost one million Allied troops had been landed in Normandy. German land forces, though still very powerful, were at the mercy of constant Allied air attack and huge numbers of German vehicles fell prey to rocket-firing fighter bombers. On 9 July, after much bitter fighting, Caen fell. Nine days later, the Americans took St Lo.

Probably the most momentous event of July, however, was the abortive attempt to assassinate Hitler. His mistrust of the army was heightened and many senior officers were executed, whether or not they were involved in the plot. The most important of these officers was Generalfeldmarschall Rommel, who was forced to commit suicide to avoid a public show trial.

On 3 September, Brussels was liberated by British troops and one day later, Antwerp was also taken. German attempts to bring London to its knees by the use of the V-2 supersonic ballistic rocket started on 8 September but, although considerable damage was done, there was no real chance that this weapon could now have any effect on the outcome of the war. By the middle of the month, US troops had crossed the German border and Allied airborne troops had landed at Arnhem in an attempt to capture the bridge over the Rhine. Unfortunately, the British paratroopers who landed at Arnhem were dropped

SS-Sturmbannführer Leon Degrelle, one of the principal figures of the Belgian Walloon 'Rexist' movement pre-war, was one of Hitler's favourites and commanded the SS-Sturmbrigade 'Wallonie'. (Josef Charita)

SS-Waffen-Unterscharführer Remi Schrijnen, one of the few Belgian Knight's Cross winners. Of interest is the reversed runes decal on the side of his M35 pattern helmet. (Chris Ailsby/Remi Schrijnen)

right into the clutches of SS-General Bittrich's Panzer Troops and, despite a spirited attempt at fulfilling their tasks, were ultimately defeated by sheer weight of numbers.

All this time, the air war against Germany carried on unabated. On 6 March, Berlin had suffered its first major Allied daylight raid when over 700 bombers attacked. Later that month, however, an Allied raid on Nuremberg suffered heavy casualties with German night fighters shooting down over 90 bombers. Mid-October saw the RAF raids on the Sorpe dam and in the middle of the following month RAF bombers scored a further success when they sank the battleship *Tirpitz* using super-heavy bombs. The last of Germany's capital ships was now gone.

In December, Hitler launched his last great gamble of the war when, on the 16th, he mounted a surprise counter-offensive through the Ardennes. Initial success was impressive as the German Panzer armies swept aside opposition in their attempt to reach the River Meuse. Bad weather prevented the Allied air forces from being brought into play. Lack of fuel supplies and the spirited defence put up by many Allied units soon slowed down the offensive well short of its targets.

In 1944, around 2448 Knight's Crosses were awarded, together with some 326 Oakleaves and 76 Swords.

SS-HAUPTSTURMFÜHRER MICHAEL WITTMANN

Michael Wittmann was born in Vogelthal, Oberpfalz, on 22 April 1914, the son of local farmer Johann Wittmann. After his schooling was completed, Wittmann worked with his father for a while before joining, in February 1934, the Freiwilligen Arbeitsdienst, in which he served until July of that year. In October 1934, Wittmann joined Infanterie Regiment 19, serving with the unit until September 1936, leaving with the rank of Gefreiter.

Wittmann was already a trained soldier, therefore, with two years of military service, when on 1 April 1937, just before his twenty third birthday, he enlisted in the SS. He joined the elite *Leibstandarte SS Adolf Hitler* and was trained at the famous Lichterfelde Barracks in Berlin. The quality and severity of the training easily matched that undergone by the Imperial Cadets of the Kaiser's day who had trained at the same barracks. This training was undoubtedly instrumental in moulding Wittmann into such a fine soldier.

By the outbreak of war in 1939, Wittmann held the rank of SS-Unterscharführer. Wittmann took part in the *Blitzkrieg* against Poland and the assault in the West. As a commander of one of the first assault guns allocated to the *Leibstandarte*, he proved himself a conscientious and competent soldier.

The invasion of the Soviet Union saw the *Leibstandarte* heading in a south-easterly direction under the command of XIV Panzer Korps. The assault guns were soon in action against strong enemy opposition. Wittmann was to become well known amongst his comrades for his coolness in action as he cautiously stalked his opponents. On 12 July 1941, he was awarded the Iron Cross Second Class. Only two months later, this was followed by the First Class. He also qualified for the Panzer Assault Badge and the Wound Badge.

In one of Wittmann's early actions on the Eastern Front, he was personally responsible for the destruction of six enemy tanks. His leadership potential was clear to his superiors and in July 1942, he was sent to the SS Junkerschule at Bad Tölz in Bavaria for officer training. Having successfully completed his training, he was commissioned in December and returned to his unit with the rank of SS-Untersturmführer.

At the start of 1943, Wittmann exchanged his Sturmgeschutze assault gun for the formidable weapon with which he was to become the world's most successful tank commander, the dreaded Tiger tank. Wittmann's prowess with the assault gun was to be completely overshadowed by his skill with this legendary weapon and his personal score began to rise steadily. In the great Panzer battles at Kursk, he claimed eight enemy tanks and seven artillery pieces on the first day alone. By the end of this offensive, Wittmann had added 30 tanks and 28 guns to his ever growing score.

Such prowess would not go unrewarded for long. On one day in late Autumn 1943, Wittmann knocked out ten enemy tanks in a single engagement, bringing his score to 66. This brought him the award of the Knight's Cross on 13 January. Wittmann's friends were amazed that it had taken so long for him to receive the recognition he so richly deserved. Tank warfare is a terrifying and confusing thing at the best of times: for one tank crew to survive

long enough to amass such a phenomenal score was itself an amazing feat.

Wittmann's scoring was by no means finished, however, and only three weeks later, he had increased his score to 88 enemy tanks. This time, however, recognition was quick in coming. On 30 January, Hitler made Wittmann the 380th recipient of the coveted Oakleaves. His gunner, SS-Rottenführer Balthasar Woll had also been awarded the Knight's Cross two weeks earlier, on 16 January. Hitler sent Wittmann the following personal telegram:

In thankful appreciation of your heroic actions in the battle for the future of our people, I award you as the 380th soldier of the German Wehrmacht, the Oakleaves to the Knight's Cross of the Iron Cross. Adolf Hitler.

Wittmann also received a much deserved promotion, to SS-Obersturmführer. He was now the commander of SS *schwere* Panzer Abteilung 501. This was the *Leibstandarte's* own heavy tank unit.

It was during the Allied invasion of Normandy a few months later in June 1944 that Wittmann was to earn his place in history. Wittmann's name has become so much linked with his tank that one can hardly mention the name of the Tiger tank without immediately thinking of Wittmann. The Tiger tank was of course a formidable weapon and many Allied units accepted that if they met up with a single Tiger, they would expect to have to put in at least three or four Shermans against it and would probably lose all but perhaps one. The frontal armour of the Tiger was so thick that Allied tank shells would merely bounce off. It was not, however, without faults. It was overheavy for its powerplant, resulting in low speed and poor manoeuvrability. In the hands of an expert such as Wittmann, however, it was an awesome weapon, as the invading Allied troops were about to discover.

On 13 June, elements of the 7 Armoured Division were advancing towards Caen as part of an attempt to outflank the defenders. Wittmann, with four other Tigers of 2 Kompanie of *schwere* Panzer Abteilung 501, was concealed on Hill 213 near the village of Villers Bocage, having already knocked out some British Cromwell tanks in the town. As the lead elements of 7 Armoured Division progressed along the sunken road typical of this Bocage area of France, Wittmann knocked out the half-track at the tail of the column. Having thus blocked any retreat for the remainder of the column, he proceeded to make his way along the column destroying every vehicle in it. British tanks fired at him in vain, their weapons useless against the Tiger's armour. Wittmann added 25 armoured vehicles to his score in this single engagement. His luck ran out shortly afterwards when his tank was disabled by a British anti-tank gun, but Wittmann and his crew escaped unharmed.

A few days later, on 22 June 1944, Wittmann was awarded the Swords to his Knight's Cross, the award being recommended personally by the *Leibstandarte's* commander, SS-Obergruppenführer und Panzergeneral der Waffen-SS Josef Dietrich. His recent successes had increased Wittmann's score to 138 tanks and 132 guns. He was also promoted to the rank of SS-Hauptsturmführer.

As with many highly decorated soldiers, Wittmann was then offered a staff posting as an instructor at a training school where his expertise could be put to good use in teaching others. Wittmann refused, preferring to stay with his comrades. It was a decision which was to cost him his life.

On 8 August 1944, Wittmann was ordered, with his Tigers, to take Cintheaux, thus protecting the flank of 12 SS Panzer Division *Hitlerjugend* to which he was temporarily attached. Wittmann's force came under heavy artillery fire but emerged unscathed to engage Sherman tanks advancing towards Cintheaux. In the battle which followed, Wittmann engaged several Shermans, knocking out three. The combined fire of five others attacking him from three sides at once finally knocked out his Tiger. There were no survivors. Wittman's resting place remained unknown until 1983 when a road widening operation uncovered his remains. He now rests in the German military cemetery at La Cambe.

Michael Wittmann was the most successful tank commander in history and had the signal honour of being awarded the Knight's Cross, Oakleaves and Swords all within the space of five months. Wittmann was an earnest man, quiet and thoughtful. He was highly admired and esteemed by his comrades and very highly thought of by his superiors. His personal bravery is unquestionable and his place in the annals of military history thoroughly deserved.

SS-HAUPTSTURMFÜHRER HANS-JOACHIM RUHLE VON LILIENSTERN

Born in Luttich in January 1915, Hans-Joachim Ruhle von Lilienstern was the son of a doctor. He attended Gymnasium and, after gaining his leaving certificate, carried on his academic studies, qualifying for his diploma in political economics in 1938. At the outbreak of war, he was serving as a reservist Leutnant and was decorated with the Iron Cross Second Class during the French Campaign, in which he served as a platoon commander.

The second year of the war in the East found him with the rank of SS-Hauptsturmführer and commander of 1 Bataillon, SS-Freiwilligen Panzer-Grenadier-Regiment 48 *General Seyffardt*. This regiment was part of 23 SS-Freiwilligen Panzer-Grenadier Division *Nederland* and was composed mostly of Dutch volunteers. With this unit he was awarded the Iron Cross First Class for actions on the Leningrad Front. On 12 February 1944, the award of the Knight's Cross of the Iron Cross followed for his gallantry and leadership on the Eastern Front.

During the summer of that year, the division was crippled at Narwa and retreated into Riga. It was eventually evacuated from Lithuania and committed to the fighting in Pomerania in 1945, surrendering to the Red Army at Furstenwalde in April. Prof. Dr Hans-Joachim Ruhle von Lilienstern survived the war and died in retirement at his Frankfurt home in 1983.

SS-HAUPTSTURMFÜHRER HEINRICH SCHMELZER

Heinrich Schmelzer was born in Nesselroden in March 1914 and joined the SS in 1935, seeing service in the Polish, French and Balkan Campaigns before the invasion of the Soviet Union.

In December 1943, he was serving with the SS Pioniere Kompanie of the Panzerkampfgruppe *Das Reich*. In late December, a Soviet offensive in the Zhitomir area succeeded in throwing back the opposing German forces and capturing the only bridge over the River Teterew in the area. *Das Reich* Panzerkampfgruppe had been on the wrong side of the river and was cut off with no escape route.

Schmelzer and his combat engineers were tasked to construct a temporary bridge to allow the Kampfgruppe to escape. Under cover of darkness on 24 December, Schmelzer and his men set to work. Despite heavy enemy fire, by 02.30 hours the following morning, Schmelzer had completed his task and the Kampfgruppe started to cross. By dawn, a full Panzer battalion, artillery and mortar battalions, an infantry regiment and all the support elements had crossed. Schmelzer and his combat engineers defended their bridge until every last vehicle and all the personnel of the Kampfgruppe had crossed.

Schmelzer's achievement had saved the Kampfgruppe from total annihilation and in recognition he was awarded the Knight's Cross on 12 March 1944 and promoted to the rank of SS-Hauptsturmführer.

SS-Hauptsturmführer Hans-Joachim Rühle von Lilienstern. Von Lilienstern is wearing other ranks pattern collar patches devoid of the normal silver cord piping found on the normal officers insignia. This was quite a common occurrence. (Arthur Charlton)

SS-Hauptsturmführer Heinrich Schmelzer, Commander of 2 (Pioniere) Kompanie of the Das Reich Kampfgruppe, Eastern Front in March 1944. (Heinrich Schmelzer)

During the Ardennes Offensive in December 1944, Schmelzer's engineers together with the Grenadier Regiment *Deutschland* had been cut off by an American tank thrust near Magoure. Schmelzer was instrumental in leading the break out and brought all the encircled German troops back to their own lines without major loss. For this, he was decorated with the Oakleaves on 28 February 1945. Schmelzer survived the war, retiring to his home town where he died in 1985.

SS-OBERSTURMBANNFÜHRER OTTO WEIDINGER

Otto Weidinger was born in Würzburg on 27 May 1914 and was to become one of only 23 Waffen-SS soldiers to win the coveted Swords to the Knight's Cross. After attending Gymnasium in Würzburg, Weidinger volunteered for the SS in April 1934 and commenced his officer training at the SS Junkerschule Braunschweig in May 1935. He was commissioned in April 1936 with the rank of SS-Untersturmführer and posted as a platoon commander in III Kompanie, SS-Standarte *Deutschland* in Ellwangen. From 3 to 29 May 1936, Weidinger attended a course of combat engineer training with the SS-Pioniere Bataillon in Ellwangen, and a Kampfschule course in Au.

Otto Weidinger took part in the occupation of Austria with the *Deutschland*

Standarte and on 11 September 1938 was promoted to SS-Obersturmführer. He served for three months on attachment to an army unit in Weingarten. On returning from this attachment, he was first appointed as adjutant to the Kradschützenbataillon in Ellwangen, then, in June 1939, as Abteilungs adjutant to the Aufklärungsabteilung.

On the outbreak of war in 1939, Weidinger was still serving with the Aufklärungsabteilung and took part in the invasion of Poland where he was appointed to command the armoured car company of the Panzer Aufklärungs abteilung on 1 November. Two weeks later, he was decorated with the Iron Cross Second Class. On 25 July 1940, during the French Campaign, he received the Iron Cross First Class and was shortly afterwards appointed to the staff of the SS-Verfügungsdivision serving in Holland and was made Divisional Adjutant later that year.

Weidinger was promoted to SS-Hauptsturmführer in July 1940 and served in that rank during the Balkan Campaign of 1941. On 22 June 1941 Hauptsturmführer Weidinger was sent into action on the central sector of the Russian Front where, in mid-July, he was given command of *schwer* Kradschützen Kompanie of the Kradschützenbataillon. Subsequently, he also commanded 1 Kompanie of the battalion before returning to the SS Junkerschule Braunschweig where he took up an appointment as a tactics instructor.

Promoted to Sturmbannführer on his return from front line duties in June 1943, he was appointed to take command of 1 Battaillon, SS Regiment *Deutschland* in the southern sector of the Eastern Front. Thrown into the thick of the fighting for the Kursk salient in July 1943, Weidinger was wounded in the lung. The regiment itself suffered heavy casualties. Thereafter, *Deutschland* was involved in the see-sawing battles back and forth across Russia as numerous Soviet assaults were met and pushed back only to be replaced by fresh attacks. In mid-August, Weidinger was again severely wounded, by grenade splinters during close quarter fighting. On 26 November 1943, Otto Weidinger was decorated with the German Cross in Gold for his gallantry and leadership during this period.

At the end of 1943, the *Das Reich* Division was reformed as a fully-fledged Panzer division. Whilst the bulk of the division was sent to the West for this refit and reformation, Weidinger became commander of SS Panzergrenadier Regiment *Das Reich* as part of SS Panzer Kampfgruppe *Das Reich*. The Kampfgruppe remained on the Eastern Front where it was involved in the Cherkassy pocket as part of the rearguard which held the line allowing other units to escape. In April 1944, the bulk of this Kampfgruppe joined the division at Bordeaux whilst Weidinger and a smaller group remained once again on the Eastern Front where it was heavily engaged in combat around Tarnopol. For his command of this smaller Kampfgruppe and his own personal gallantry during this period, Weidinger was decorated with the Knight's Cross of the Iron Cross on 21 April 1944. He was also awarded the Close Combat Clasp during this period.

On 14 June 1944 Weidinger was appointed to command SS Panzergrenadier Regiment *Der Führer* on the Western Front. During the invasion battles in

A fine photograph of SS-Obersturmbannführer Otto Weidinger which clearly shows his Swords and Oakleaves. To the right can be seen the 'DF' monogram of his Regiment **Der Führer** *and the* insignia of the **Das Reich** Division. *(Otto Weidinger)*

Normandy, *Der Führer* was in action north of St Lo where it engaged US Army units and was eventually encircled at Coutances. Succeeding in breaking out from this entrapment, *Der Führer* took part in the attack on Mortain but eventually had to retreat and escaped through the Falaise Gap to cross the Seine, reaching the safety of the West Wall in September.

Der Führer subsequently saw action in the Ardennes Offensive as part of 'Sepp' Dietrich's 6 Panzerarmee on the northern flank, as a reserve. Committed to battle on 19 December as part of von Manteuffel's force attacking US airborne troops at St Vith, *Der Führer* very nearly succeeded in reaching the River Meuse but was to suffer terrible casualties when the improvement in weather conditions allowed the Allies to bring their air forces into action. Weidinger was awarded the Oakleaves on 28 December in recognition of his command of the regiment during the Normandy and Ardennes battles.

On 6 March 1945, the *Das Reich* Division was thrown into the battle for Hungary where the German armies were fighting a withdrawal in the face of overwhelming Soviet forces. The Germans withdrew into Austria and by 5 April, *Das Reich* was in action in the battle for Vienna. *Der Führer* was further involved in Hungary in suppressing the insurrection in Prague before withdrawing westwards and surrendering to US forces on 9 May at Rokyczany near Pilsen. Just three days before the surrender, Otto Weidinger became the 150th recipient of the Swords.

After the end of the war, all officers of the *Das Reich* Division were taken into custody and screened to establish any possible responsibility for the killings at

Tulle and Oradour during the march of the division from the south of France to the Normandy battlefields. Otto Weidinger was completely exonerated of any complicity in these matters and was released in 1951. These events forever cast a shadow over the division's achievements. Otto Weidinger has made a study of the Tulle and Oradour tragedies using evidence from both German and French sources and has produced a book *Tulle and Oradour — A Franco-German Tragedy*.

Otto Weidinger has also written the definitive history of the 2 SS Panzer Division, *Division Das Reich* (Munin Verlag, Osnabrück) and was elected Honorary President of the division's veterans' organisation in April 1983.

SS-HAUPTSTURMFÜHRER WILLI HEIN

Born on 26 April 1917 as the son of a decorator in Schleswig-Holstein, Willi Hein served in the Reichsarbeitsdienst from April to October 1939 after which time he volunteered for service with the SS and was accepted into the Freiwilligen Grenadier Regiment *Nordland*.

In 1942, Hein was commissioned as an SS-Untersturmführer after attending the SS Junkerschule at Bad Tölz. After commissioning, he was posted to the Eastern Front to join 5 SS Panzer Regiment *Wiking* as a Troop Commander. Hein saw much fierce combat with the Panzer Regiment of what was to become one of the best of the Waffen-SS divisions, with a fighting reputation second to none. Hein received a Führer-Commendation for his service in the battles around Kharkov in August 1943. He had his name entered in the Roll of Honour of the German army in November of the same year and received the German Cross in Gold in June 1944.

In the summer of 1944, the *Wiking* Division had been committed to battle in the Tscherkassy cauldron. At Olschana, the divisional supply lines had been overrun by strong Soviet forces. Obersturmführer Hein was given the task of counter-attacking and duly set off into the night with a mere two hastily repaired assault guns and some two dozen men. Despite his meagre forces, Hein succeeded in throwing back the Soviets, destroying three T-34 tanks and capturing over two hundred enemy prisoners. Hein was awarded the Knight's Cross in recognition of his achievement. The award was made on 4 May 1944.

On 30 January 1945, Hein was promoted to the rank of SS-Hauptsturmführer. Hein ended the war in hospital, having been seriously wounded in action during combat in Budapest. He survived the war and now lives in retirement in his native Schleswig-Holstein.

OBERST HERMANN HADERECKER

Hermann Haderecker was born in April 1915, and in 1944 was serving with Grenadier Regiment 20, part of 10 Panzergrenadier Division, originally an infantry division of the old Reichswehr. After serving in France, Poland and the Balkans, the division spent the remainder of the war on the Eastern Front.

The SS-pattern black Panzerjacke and officers peaked cap are shown to good effect in this fine shot of SS-Obersturmführer Willi Hein, from SS Panzer Regiment 5 Wiking. (Willi Hein)

Oberst Hermann Haderecker, shown here as a Major commanding Grenadier Regiment 20. Clearly seen amongst Haderecker's awards are the Knight's Cross, Honour Roll Clasp, Close Combat Clasp and Bronze Infantry Assault Badge. (Hermann Haderecker)

Haderecker was decorated with the German Cross in April 1942 during the defensive battles following the 1941/42 Soviet winter offensive. On the southern sector of the front, the division was heavily mauled during the battle for Kiev in autumn 1943. By early 1944, the division had been so badly battered that it had a total strength of only 3700 men to cover a ten-mile long stretch of front line. For his personal gallantry and leadership during these difficult times, Haderecker was decorated with the Knight's Cross on 4 May 1944.

Grenadier Regiment 20 was the only remaining main combat unit of the division by late 1944, casualties having forced the disbandment of its other components. The remnants of the division surrendered to Soviet forces in Czechoslovakia at the end of the war.

Oberst Haderecker survived the war and now lives in retirement.

MAJOR WALTER VON WIETERSHEIM

Born in November 1917, Walter von Wietersheim served as Commander of II/Panzer Regiment *Grossdeutschland*, with the rank of Hauptmann, in May

1944 when *Grossdeutschland* was heavily involved in defensive actions on the Eastern Front. Still a very powerful formation despite gruelling years of war and heavy losses, the division was being used in rearguard actions to cover the withdrawal of retreating units. The division carried out its tasks so successfully that it was even able to go on to counter-attack the Soviets in some areas.

As the Soviet forces closed in on the Rumanian town of Jassy, *Grossdeutschland* found itself in a perfect position for a flank attack on the enemy. This was a great success and the Soviet forces were forced right back through the town of Targual Framas and beyond. This could only be a temporary respite, however, and strong Soviet forces were eventually to push back the *Grossdeutschland* units and gather for a massed offensive. Aware of this, *Grossdeutschland*'s Panzer units pre-empted the Soviet attack with a surprise attack which resulted in the destruction of much Soviet equipment. A further Soviet attack was launched in late April but after a few days fighting, this was also halted with heavy Soviet losses by the might of *Grossdeutschland*'s formidable Tiger and Panther tanks.

On 2 May, a further Soviet attack was launched. Once again, the weary troops of the German army's premiere elite formation were waiting. As the Soviet forces attacked, their infantry were scythed down by the waiting

Major Walter von Wietersheim, Commander of 2 Abteilung, Panzer Regiment **Grossdeutsch-land**. *This photograph was taken just after the award of Knight's Cross in May 1944. (Walter von Wietersheim)*

A fine study of SS-Oberscharführer Johann Fiedler. As well as his Knight's Cross, clearly visible is his Demjansk shield just above the sleeve eagle and the Close Combat Clasp in Silver. (Johann Fiedler)

grenadiers. This left the Soviet heavy armour with no infantry cover and *Grossdeutschland*'s carefully concealed 88mm guns ripped the Soviet tanks apart. The Tigers and Sturmgeschutzen finished the job.

Walter von Wietersheim was personally responsible for the destruction of fourteen enemy tanks, six anti-tank guns and two artillery pieces. For this achievement, he was decorated with the Knight's Cross on 15 May 1944.

SS-OBERSCHARFÜHRER JOHANN FIEDLER

Johann Fiedler was born on 28 April 1922 as the son of a shoesmith in Stangendorf, in the Sudetenland. After leaving school, he trained as a locksmith until May 1941 when, at the age of nineteen, he applied to join the Waffen-SS and was called up in Prague. After his basic training in Prague, Fiedler was posted to the 3 SS Panzer Grenadier Division *Totenkopf*.

Very soon after Fiedler's induction into the SS-*Totenkopf* Division, in which he served with SS-*Totenkopf* Regiment 3, the unit was moved to the northern sector of the front in Operation BARBAROSSA, the invasion of the Soviet Union. Fiedler was with *Totenkopf* when the division was cut off in the Demjansk cauldron. He received his first wound during this fourteen-month siege, but remained with his unit. He was decorated with the Wound Badge. Also during the Demjansk action, Fiedler was awarded the Iron Cross Second Class. Soon after the relief of the beleaguered German forces, this was followed by the award of the First Class.

After a relatively quiet couple of months in which the SS-*Totenkopf* Division got some much needed rest and reinforcements, it was soon back in the thick of the fighting again. During a fierce battle near Pascani, elements of the regiment came under fire from some concealed Soviet positions. Fiedler spotted the enemy and realised that his unit would be pinned down unless the enemy were neutralised. Storming the enemy positions with a total disregard for his own safety, he destroyed them and, despite being wounded and suffering great loss of blood, took 39 prisoners and captured a Soviet anti-tank gun and two heavy and five light machine guns.

Only through the determination and bravery of SS-Unterscharführer Fiedler was the progress of his unit able to continue. He was awarded the Knight's Cross of the Iron Cross in recognition of his gallantry on 16 June 1944. The award was made personally by SS-Gruppenführer and Generalleutnant der Waffen-SS Hermann Preiss at the Divisional Headquarters. With the decoration came a promotion when, one week later, he was elevated to the rank of SS-Oberscharführer.

In December 1944, whilst serving with a combat group near Frankfurt on the Oder, he was captured by Soviet troops. He managed to escape, however, and reached German lines in January 1945. Shortly afterwards, Fiedler was serving on the Western Front and he went into American captivity after the surrender in May 1945.

After the war, Johann Fiedler returned to his pre-war trade as a locksmith. He died in 1985.

OBERFELDWEBEL FRANZ SIEBERT

Born in Gelsenkirchen on 17 March 1915, Franz Siebert served with 3 Kompanie/Panzerjäger Abteilung 306. This unit was part of 306 Infanterie Division serving on the Russian Front.*

During the latter part of 1943, 306 Infanterie Division was involved in very heavy combat north east of Kriwoi Rog. 3/Panzerjäger Abteilung was positioned near the village of Marjewka where Oberfeldwebel Siebert commanded two self-propelled guns, in position and ready to give any enemy attackers a bloody nose.

Early one morning, the Soviets attacked with armour support. Siebert's assault guns opened fire and after a short but bitter exchange, three enemy tanks lay blazing, victims of Siebert's guns. Shortly afterwards, two further Soviet tanks and a self-propelled gun started to probe towards Siebert's position. A few well placed shots later, the self-propelled gun was in flames and the tanks had retreated.

Soon, enemy infantry, some two hundred strong, were attacking, supported by yet more of the enemy's T-34 tanks. Siebert's small group redoubled their efforts and took out two more enemy tanks in quick succession. Now, however, his ammunition was beginning to run low and he rapidly withdrew nearer to the edge of the village to avoid any attempt to encircle him. The battle flared again and three further T-34's fell victim to his accurate gunfire.

By now Siebert's ammunition was exhausted but this did not deter him. Dismounted, he stormed towards the enemy throwing hand grenades and opening fire with his machine pistol. The enemy was held off long enough for the two assault guns to safely withdraw.

This brave NCO was a shining example of cool-headed daring, a typical experienced East Front fighter who knew how to keep his head in a tight situation when facing superior enemy forces. For his successful destruction of so many enemy tanks during this fierce battle, Oberfeldwebel Siebert was awarded the Knight's Cross on 9 July 1944.

OBERFELDWEBEL HERMANN BUCHNER

Buchner was born in Salzburg, Austria, in October 1919 and commenced his flying career in November 1941 when he passed through the fighter pilot school in Werneuchen. Oberfeldwebel Buchner served on the Eastern Front with the same squadron as Stuka ace Hans Ulrich Rudel, Schlachtgeschwader 2 *Immelmann*.

As a pilot with 6 Staffel, he flew numerous close support missions and gained a score of 46 victories. For this achievement, he was decorated with the Knight's Cross on 20 July 1944. It is interesting to note that this score, obtained

---

* In Autumn 1944, 306 Infanterie Division was so badly mauled in severe combat against overwhelming Soviet forces that it was disbanded.

Oberfeldwebel Franz Siebert, a troop commander with 3 Kompanie, Panzerjäger Abteilung 306. The small gothic 'P' motif for anti-tank troops can just be made out on the shoulder strap. (Franz Siebert)

Oberst Hermann Buchner. At the time this photograph was taken, Buchner was an Oberfeldwebel flying with Schlachtgeschwader 2 'Immelmann'. Buchner later flew in the Me 262 jet fighter. (Hermann Buchner)

by a fighter pilot on the Western Front during the earlier part of the war, would have been sufficient to warrant the award of the Oakleaves. In addition, during his period of service on the Eastern Front, Buchner destroyed forty six enemy tanks.

In November 1944, Buchner was transferred from the Eastern Front and assigned to home defence duties. By the time he left the Eastern Front, he had flown over six hundred combat missions. On his transfer, Buchner was trained to fly the superb Messerschmitt Me 262 jet fighter. He was to become one of the most successful of the jet pilots, shooting down twelve enemy aircraft with this formidable weapon.

By the end of hostilities, Oberfeldwebel Buchner had flown 640 combat missions, had shot down 58 enemy aircraft and destroyed 46 enemy tanks. He was in fact recommended for the award of the Oakleaves but the war ended before the recommendation could be processed.

Buchner survived the war and now lives in retirement in his native Austria.

SS-OBERSCHARFÜHRER ERNST BARKMANN

Ernst Barkmann was born in Kisdorf in August 1919, the son of a Holstein farmer. After leaving school in 1935, he began to learn the family business with his father, but on 1 April 1939 started his military service as a voluntee with SS-Standarte *Germania*. After three months basic training at Hamburg, h joined III Bataillon of the Standarte at Radolfszell.

During the Polish Campaign, he served with 9 Kompanie as a machine gunner and was wounded in action during house-to-house fighting. He wa wounded in action again, more seriously, during the opening phase o Operation BARBAROSSA, in action near Dnieprpetrowsk. Around this time h was also awarded the Iron Cross Second Class.

After recovering from his wounds, Barkmann spent some time as a instructor with European SS-Volunteers in Holland before returning to actio in early 1942, volunteering for service with the division's Panzer regiment.

Barkmann returned to the Russian Front in the winter of 1942, serving wit 2 Kompanie, SS Panzer Regiment 2 *Das Reich*. At this time the unit wa equipped with the PzKpfw III medium tank which was armed with the 5cm gun. In early 1943, the Panzer regiment was involved in the battle for Kharko where Barkmann won the Iron Cross First Class. After Kharkov, Barkmann' unit was re-equipped with the new PzKpfw V Panther tank, a much mor powerful weapon. Around this time Barkmann was promoted to SS Unterscharführer.

At the start of 1944, the division was located around Bordeaux in the sout of France for rest and refitting as a fully-fledged Panzer division. Following th Allied invasion of Normandy, the division was marched north and was soo committed to battle.

In early July, *Das Reich* was in combat north of St Lo to halt the advance o the US 9 and 30 Infantry Divisions and the US 3 Armoured Division. On 8 July Barkmann's Kompanie was in the spearhead of the regiment's attack on th advancing Americans. On this day Barkmann was to knock out his first Allie Sherman tank. It was to be the first of many adding to his score of Sovie Shermans.

For Barkmann and his crew, the days of the vast, open Russian Steppes ideal tank country, were over. Tank fighting in Normandy was an altogethe more hazardous and difficult task, with opposing tanks stalking each othe through this region's sunken, hedge-lined roads. Normandy also found th German tank formations under frequent heavy artillery and fighter-bombe attack so that individual tank camouflage became of the utmost importance The superiority of German tank design meant that a single skilfully conceale Panzer could wreak dreadful damage on Allied forces before being neutralised

A few days later, on 12 July, Barkmann destroyed two more Shermans an disabled a third. Then, taking advantage of a lull in the fighting, Barkmann an his crew camouflaged their Panther in a good ambush position and settle down to await the advancing enemy. On the morning of the following day Barkmann spotted movement behind a hedgerow. He ordered his gunlayer t load with armour piercing shot and traversed the turret in the direction of th movement. Soon, six Shermans appeared and Barkmann opened fire with th Panther's deadly 75mm gun. The lead Sherman was hit and smoke poure from its hatch. Two more kills quickly followed.

Nearby, Panzer grenadiers warned Barkmann that some Americans had go

SS-Oberscharführer Ernst Barkmann, one of Germany's great Panzer aces of the Normandy battlefields. Of particular note in this photograph is the use of buttons with an SS Totenkopf motif on the shoulder straps along with the regimental number 2. (Ernst Schmuck-Barkmann)

Ernst Barkmann in the turret of his Panther '401'. He wears the camouflage tank overalls worn by many SS tank crewmen at this stage in the war. The design of the commander's cupola indicates that this is an early Panther model D. (Ernst Schmuck-Barkmann)

Barkmann's powerful Panther tank was more than a match for any tank the Allies could field during the Normandy Campaign. It was armed with a 75mm gun and was very well armoured. (Ernst Schmuck-Barkmann)

into position behind him. His Panther moved off quickly and, crashing through a small wood, surprised the Americans. Firing high explosive ammunition Barkmann soon neutralised one American anti-tank gun but his Panther was hit by two shots from another. The first merely bounced off, but the second hit the turret and caused a fire. Barkmann decided to abandon the tank but, once outside, realised that the gunlayer had not escaped the burning vehicle. Barkmann re-entered the tank and pulled him free. The crew were able to tackle the fire and succeeded in putting out the flames. The Panther was returned to the workshops for repair.

Early next morning, 14 July, Barkmann was tasked with recovering four of the unit's Panthers which had been cut off behind enemy lines. With his own tank under repair, he was forced to use a spare. Entering the turret, he noted that blood from the previous commander, who had been killed from a head wound, still spattered the interior. Barkmann succeeded in his task, recovering the Panthers without loss. During the course of that morning, he added three more Shermans to his score.

At noon on that day, Barkmann was brought before the Regimental Commander, SS-Oberstumbannführer Tyschen, who indicated a house in which the Americans were holding some wounded German prisoners and ordered Barkmann to effect their release. Barkmann set off with three other Panthers and soon the wounded Germans were back in friendly hands. Later that day, Barkmann's Panther was damaged in an artillery barrage and his own Panther, now returned from the workshops, was given back to him.

On 26 July, Barkmann's Panther was hit by mechanical trouble when his carburettor gave out. As the mechanics furiously laboured to repair the disabled tank, stranded in the open without cover, Allied fighter-bombers attacked. The Panther's engine was hit and caught fire but luckily the flames were eventually extinguished and by dawn of the following day, the tank was once again in running order. Barkmann, however, was now cut off from the rest of the Kompanie and set out to rejoin his comrades.

On the way, near the village of le Lorey, the Panther stopped alongside some infantrymen who were running in the opposite direction. They warned Barkmann that the Americans were on the way. Two of Barkmann's men went off to verify this report and soon returned, one wounded. The Americans were indeed coming. With his main and secondary armament cleared for battle, Barkmann proceeded up the road until he reached a crossroads where he stopped the Panther, well screened by the high banks and a large oak tree.

As the enemy column approached, Barkmann opened fire. The road was soon littered with blazing American vehicles, petrol tankers, lorries, half-tracks, jeeps and tanks. The Americans called up tactical fighter support and soon the lone Panther was at the receiving end of a very nasty bombardment from bombs and tank shells. The Panther lost a track, and Barkmann's driver was wounded. Bomb damage had also jammed both the driver's and radio operator's hatches, trapping them inside.

As things became more serious, Barkmann's driver skilfully managed to steer the crippled Panther away on its one remaining track into the village of Neufbourg, where the driver and radio operator were released. Amongst the many enemy vehicles accounted for during the battle were no less than nine Sherman tanks.

Barkmann reached Coutances on 28 July. By this time he had destroyed fifteen Sherman tanks in just two days of fighting. Crossing the Seine, he reached Granville that afternoon. Two days later, the Americans had succeeded in surrounding Granville but Barkmann, towing another disabled Panther, managed to break out. Later abandoning this disabled tank, the crew set it on fire. Unfortunately, it was too close to Barkmann's Panther which also caught fire and was lost. Barkmann and his men now had to make their way to the German lines on foot, across seven kilometres of the shallows by Avranches, reaching their own lines on 5 August.

News of Barkmann's exploits had already reached his regiment and he had been recommended for the Knight's Cross. The award was approved on 27 August and the decoration itself awarded on 5 September.

Barkmann's successful career continued and he saw action again during the Ardennes Offensive where he once again served with distinction. On 25 December, he was wounded in the head by a shell splinter. Recovering consciousness, Barkmann found himself in a tent with a label on his chest indicating his destination as a hospital near Cologne. Barkmann calmly lifted the plaster on the back of his head, pulled out the shrapnel from his wound, and hitching a lift from a motorcyclist of the regiment, reported back for duty.

In March 1945, Barkmann was back in action against the Soviets around the town of Stuhlweissenburg. Here Barkmann knocked out four Russian T-34 tanks, bringing the total score of the *Das Reich* Division for the war so far to 3,000 enemy tanks destroyed! The once mighty *Das Reich* Division was being slowly decimated in continuous action. Breaking out from a Soviet encirclement in the second half of March, Barkmann's Abteilung had only nine combat-worthy tanks and three of these were subsequently lost in action against some of the new Soviet Josef Stalin heavy tanks. The remaining six Panthers finally linked up with the remnants of the Panzer regiment of the *Leibstandarte* under SS-Standartenführer Jochen Peiper.

By April 1945, Barkmann was in action south of Vienna during the battle for Austria. Leading a troop of three Panthers towards the Regimental HQ, his tank was hit by a Panzerfaust anti-tank bazooka fired by a German NCO who had mistaken Barkmann's Panzers for Soviet vehicles. Barkmann suffered a number of abdominal wounds and arm wounds from small slivers of shrapnel. The gunlayer was blinded in both eyes and the radio operator also received numerous splinter wounds. After leaving his wounded comrades with some medics, Barkmann continued on his way, only to have his Panther slide into a huge bomb crater from which it could not be retrieved and it had to be destroyed. Barkmann fortunately survived these hectic final days of the war, and succeeded in making his way west where he was taken into British captivity.

A brave and very successful tank soldier, Ernst Barkmann bears the Knight's Cross as of right, earned by his daring and unselfish gallantry. His other decorations include the rare Panzer Assault Badges for 25 and 50 engagements with the enemy. Barkmann is still alive and the author is grateful to him for providing photographs and documentary material for use in this book.

Just visible next to the Iron Cross on Hauptmann Siegfried Keiling's breast pocket is the Eastern Peoples Award and, on his right sleeve, the arm badge of the Russian Army of Liberation. The ribbon of the Eastern Peoples Award, Second Class, is worn from the buttonhole. (Siegfried Keiling)

Oberst Heinz-Günther Guderian, Operations Officer of 116 Panzer Division, wearing the special pattern collar patches for Staff Officers on his double-breasted assault gun jacket. (Heinz-Günther Guderian)

HAUPTMANN SIEGFRIED KEILING

Siegfried Keiling was born into a good middle class Berlin family on 28 October 1911. His father, August Keiling, was a leading service engineer in the Seimens-Schuckert-Werke. As a serving army officer, Siegfried Keiling was somewhat protected from the political indoctrination of the times, though he flirted with the Reichsbanner, one of the more respectable political organisations of those times.

By mid-1941, Keiling was a staff officer with 134 Artillerie Regiment when the unit crossed into Russia during Operation BARBAROSSA. In common with most other German soliders, Keiling had little or no knowledge of Russia, its people or its customs. He was soon in action and by the end of 1941, and the start of the first Russian winter of the Eastern Campaign, Keiling had been wounded in action and had been decorated with the Iron Cross Second Class.

In the summer of 1942, Keiling was transferred to command an Artillerie Abteilung composed of Russian volunteers, most of whom had only recently been in the Red Army fighting against the Germans. Like many Russians, they had no love for the Soviet system and were only too willing to fight for the Germans. Despite the misgivings of many Germans about the reliability and battle-worthiness of the Russian volunteers, Keiling's troops were soon in action and fought successfully in anti-partisan operations before being transferred to the Western Front in 1944.

The Allied invasion of France in June 1944 saw Keiling's Artillerie Abteilung ready for action but once again higher command showed grave doubts about their use in battle. The serious situation at the front soon required the use of all available troops, however, and Keiling's confidence in his volunteers was soon to be put to the test. Before long, his horse-drawn artillery was in action against US armoured units. A number of American tanks were destroyed during the Abteilung's baptism of fire and the success that the unit had achieved helped to weld the Abteilung's German and Russian troops into a tight-knit, efficient fighting unit.

After disengaging from the steadily advancing Allied forces, the Russian volunteers withdrew in a forced march toward the rear. Under constant attack, the Russians nevertheless came through this difficult period well. The Russians loved their horses and lavished great care and attention on them. Casualties through enemy action could not be avoided but no horse fell through exhaustion or maltreatment. The Russians were great scavengers and no French farmer's hidden hordes of oats or carrots were safe when the welfare of the Russians' horses was at stake. The Abteilung continued their fighting withdrawal through France and Belgium, steadily increasing their score as they went.

In September 1944, Keiling's troops were ordered to take and hold a crossing over the Schelde to allow the remnants of his retreating Armeegruppe to cross. Knowing the importance of his task and the seriousness of the situation, Keiling and his men set to their task without waiting for infantry support. Against heavy artillery fire and tank attacks, Keiling steadfastly held his position, his forces stretched to the limit and bolstered with whatever stragglers could be found. For 24 hours Keiling held his position, his personal gallantry and leadership an example to his men.

Hitler awarded Keiling the Knight's Cross on 4 October 1944. Keiling was to state that he wore the award in proud commemoration of the fallen German and Russian comrades of Ost-Artillerie-Abteilung 621. This Knight's Cross was Keiling's answer to all who doubted the reliability of his Russian troops.

Keiling survived the war and in 1957 formed the Deutsch-Russlandische Gesellschaft. He is still alive today.

OBERST HEINZ-GÜNTHER GUDERIAN

Born in August 1914, Heinz-Günther Guderian was to follow in the footsteps of his famous father, Generaloberst Guderian, Inspector General of Panzertruppe and one of Germany's finest soldiers. Guderian commenced his military career in 1933 when he joined Kraftfahrabteilung 3. He became an Officer Cadet in 1935 and was commissioned as a Leutnant with Panzer Regiment 1 in Erfurt.

He saw service in both the Polish and Western Campaigns and during the invasion of the Soviet Union was attached to III Armee Korps south of Rostov, for General Staff Training. In 1942, he was attached to the Kriegsakademie and was thereafter employed on the staff of 11 Panzer Division and III Panzer Korps.

In 1943, Guderian transferred to the staff of 116 Panzer Division and, during the Normandy battles, by this time an Oberst, was the senior Operations Officer. Held in reserve in case of a second invasion force attacking, the division was not committed to battle until late in July. It tood part in the abortive counter-attack near Mortain in early August and was trapped in the Falaise Pocket near Argentan later that month.

During the night of 20/21 August, Guderian led a group of three hundred or so men and 50 vehicles in a night breakout from the pocket. After hours of agonisingly slow progress, his group finally established contact with men of the *Das Reich* Panzer Division who were holding the German front line in the area.

The following day, Guderian was travelling in a staff car which came under attack from an Allied fighter-bomber. Severely wounded, he was evacuated to a field hospital and whilst recovering from his wounds, he was visited by his father, who personally presented his son with the Knight's Cross of the Iron Cross for his part in the successful breakout from the Falaise Pocket.

Oberst Guderian survived the war and returned to the service of his country in the Federal Republic's Bundeswehr. He became General der Kampftruppe in 1974 and was to reach the rank of Generalmajor before retiring. In the tradition of this illustrious family, both of Guderian's sons are serving with the West German Army.

SS-STURMBANNFÜHRER ERNST-AUGUST KRAG

Ernst-August Krag was born on 20 February 1915 in Wiesbaden. He joined the SS in May 1935 and was posted to 5 Kompanie of the *Germania* Standarte in Arolsen. Krag also had the distinction of being one of Germany's first paratroopers, qualifying from the Paratroop Training School at Stendal. In 1938, Krag was sent to the SS Junkerschule at Bad Tölz and after completing his training successfully, was commissioned with the rank of SS-Untersturmführer in 1939. Krag was to specialise in the Artillery branch of the Waffen-SS and attended the Artillery School in Jüterbog before taking up the position of battery Observation Officer in 5 Batterie/Artillerie Regiment *Das Reich*.

Progressing from traditional artillery to the powerful and deadly self-propelled gun battalion, in 1942 Krag became commander of 2 Kompanie of the *Das Reich* Division's Sturmgeschützabteilung and in the following year, commander of the Abteilung itself. By the summer of 1944, Krag was in command of the Division's Panzer Aufklärungsabteilung, seeing action during the ferocious combat in Normandy. For his successful and proficient handling of the Abteilung during these battles, Krag was decorated with the Knight's Cross on 23 October 1944. In February 1945, he was awarded the Oakleaves to the Knight's Cross for his service with the Aufklärungsabteilung during the Ardennes Offensive.

Sturmbannführer Krag's other decorations included the German Cross in

Several interesting features can be seen in this exceptionally clear photograph of Oakleaves winner, SS-Sturmbannführer Ernst-August Krag including the **Das Reich** *Divisional cuffband, the rare Panzer Assault Badge for 25 engagements with the enemy and the heavy bullion wire-embroidered officers sleeve eagle. (Ernst-August Krag)*

In this photograph of Major Erich Schroedter, commanding officer of the Panzer Aufklärungs Abteilung of the elite **Grossdeutschland** *Division, the 'GD' monogram in gilt metal is just visible on the shoulder strap. (Erich Schroedter)*

Gold, the Close Combat Clasp and the rare Panzer Assault Badge for 25 engagements with the enemy. He survived the war and lived in retirement in Niederhausen until his death in 1985.

MAJOR ERICH SCHROEDTER

Erich Schroedter was born in Munich on 1 May 1919. He commenced training as an officer cadet in the Kradschützen Bataillon of 3 Panzer Division in Bad Freienwald and attended Kriegsschule in Hannover during 1938−39. August 1939 saw Schroedter commissioned as Leutnant and Platoon Commander in Kradschützen Bataillon of 8 'Schnelle' Division. He served in this capacity during the Polish Campaign, winning the Iron Cross Second Class on 5 October 1939. During the French Campaign, Schroedter served as Divisional Ordnance Officer, winning the Iron Cross First Class on 7 July 1940. Schroedter then saw service during the invasion of Jugoslavia as Adjutant in the Kradschützen Bataillon of 8 Panzer Division. In this period, he qualified for the Panzer Assault Badge in Bronze.

Taking part in the invasion of the Soviet Union in 1941, Schroedter saw intensive action and was twice severely wounded, requiring long periods of hospitalisation. In October 1941, he was promoted to Oberleutnant.

In May 1942, Schroedter was posted to Panzertruppeschule IV in Krampnit. near Potsdam. In action at the front once again later that same year, he wa. wounded yet again and awarded the Wound Badge in Silver. In the spring o 1943, Schroedter was appointed Ordnance Officer to the Chief of General Staf of the 4 Panzer Armee and promoted to Hauptmann in May.

In February 1944, Schroedter was posted as Squadron Commander to the Panzer Aufklärungsabteilung *Grossdeutschland* and was quickly back in the thick of the fighting. He again suffered severe wounds and was awarded the Wound Badge in Gold on 8 June 1944. The following month, he was awarded the German Cross in Gold. During August 1944, Hauptmann Schroedter attended a training course for Battalion Commanders of armoured reconnaissance and on 22 September was appointed Commander of Panzer Aufklärungsabteilung *Grossdeutschland*.

During the Soviet offensive in Kurland, Schroedter and his Panze Aufklärungsabteilung were at the spearhead of a German counter-attack aimed at holding the Soviet forces and freeing an encircled German force north west of Memel. Schroedter's unit acquitted itself very well, allowing the encircled Germans to escape and causing heavy Soviet losses. For thi achievement, he was awarded the Knight's Cross on 23 October 1944. On 30 January 1945, Schroedter was promoted to the rank of Major.

In mid-February 1945, Soviet forces were attempting to crush the German units around Königsberg whilst units of the Soviet 2 Byelorussian Front had swept north taking Elbing and cutting off German access to the west. The Soviets launched furious attacks on the encircled Germans. Almost impossible demands were made of the German soldier during these hectic days Schroedter's Panzer Aufklärungsabteilung was no different: time and again i launched itself at overwhelming Soviet forces and caused the enemy heavy casualties. During one ferocious engagement, Schroedter was responsible fo destroying ten enemy tanks. For his distinguished service during this phase o the battle, Major Schroedter was decorated with the Oakleaves as the 808th recipient, on 28 March 1945.

MAJOR HANS SANDROCK

Born in April 1913 in Saarbrücken, Hans Sandrock was the son of an official in the Air Ministry. He attended Volksschule and subsequently Gymnasium, in Berlin-Steglitz. After leaving school, he trained for one year as an apprentice with a crane and elevator factory in Berlin, followed by four terms study a Technical High School as a Mechanical Engineer.

On 1 September 1934, Sandrock enlisted as a volunteer in Kraftfahrlehr-Kommando Zossen near Berlin, being promoted to Gefreiter in April 1935. He was put forward as an officer aspirant. After attending the Hannover War School in 1936, he was posted to Panzer Regiment 5 and commissioned as a Leutnant.

As a Platoon Commander with 2 Kompanie, Panzer Regiment 5, Leutnan

Sandrock took part in the occupation of the Sudetenland. On 1 September 1939, he was promoted to Oberleutnant and served with 1 Kompanie, Panzer Regiment 5, during the Polish Campaign. In this period, Panzer Regiment 5 formed part of 3 Panzer Division, with Guderian's XIX Korps, attacking through northern Poland. Sandrock received the Iron Cross Second Class on 22 October 1939.

During the French Campaign, 5 Panzer Regiment distinguished itself as part of Hoepner's XVI Panzer Korps, attacking through Belgium and participating in the pursuit after the evacuation of Dunkirk. Sandrock was awarded the Panzer Assault Badge on 6 June 1940. In late 1940, 5 Panzer Regiment was removed from 3 Panzer Division and became a formation of the 5 Light Division.

On 10 March 1941, 5 Panzer Regiment was sent to North Africa as part of the elite Afrika Korps. It fought in the push to Egypt and the efforts to capture Tobruk. In the summer of 1941, it was reformed within 21 Panzer Division. In 1942, 5 Panzer Regiment shared in the capture of Benghazi, fought in the battle of Gazala and saw action during the fall of Tobruk and the push to El Alamein. During his service in North Africa, Sandrock was awarded the Iron Cross First Class in April 1941, the Italian Bravery Medal in February 1942 and the German Cross in Gold on 1 June 1942. He was promoted to the rank of

Hauptmann Sandrock wears the tropical tan-coloured **Luftwaffe** *tunic bearing the Africa campaign cuff title on the left sleeve and the Divisional* **Hermann Göring** *cuff title on the right sleeve. Partly hidden is the German Cross in Gold on the right breast pocket. (Hans Sandrock)*

Sandrock, by this point a Major, wears an interesting combination of uniform items. His cap is the standard **Luftwaffe** *officers pattern and his tunic is the Field Grey assault gun pattern, and he wears a black Panzer shirt. (Hans Sandrock)*

Hauptmann on 1 April 1942. Late that year, 21 Panzer Division was badly mauled in heavy fighting when the British launched Operation SUPERCHARGE on 1 November. Hauptmann Sandrock was severely wounded and wa returned to Germany for hospital treatment and recuperation.

On 25 July 1943, Hauptmann Sandrock, fully recovered, was posted to another elite unit, Fallschirmpanzerregiment *Hermann Göring*, and served with III (Sturmgeschutz) Abteilung during the fighting withdrawal through Sicily and the evacuation to the Italian mainland over the Straits of Messina. The *Hermann Göring* Panzer Regiment fought in all the major battles in Italy. In May 1944, it was sent to Leghorn in the north of Italy and temporarily held in reserve. However, the breakout of the Allies from the beachead at Anzio soon saw *Hermann Göring* being rushed back into action again and it remained in front line service until after the fall of Rome. The division was then transferred to the Eastern Front where it became part of the force Model was assembling to counter the Soviet armies advancing on Warsaw.

Sandrock was awarded the Panzer Assault Badge for 25 engagements on December 1943, and the following grade, for 50 engagements, in June 1944 Around this time, the division was successful in its participation in the destruction of the Soviet III Tank Corps near Warsaw.

On 18 October 1944, Sandrock was promoted to Major. *Hermann Göring* a the time was engaged in furious fighting in East Prussia where, on 20–2. October it succeeded in throwing back the Soviet II Guards Army a Nemersdorf. During this battle, Sandrock's personal score of enemy tanks an armoured vehicles destroyed reached 123. For this achievement, Sandrock wa decorated with the Knight's Cross of the Iron Cross on 21 October. Hi decoration, and with it the *Luftwaffe* Salver of Honour, were presented b General der Artillerie Weidlich, Commander of XXXI Panzer Korps. Wounded in action during April 1945, Sandrock was again hospitalised and on hi recovery, joined the *Hermann Göring* reserve Abteilung in Orianenburg Although the bulk of the *Hermann Göring* units were cut off and captured b Soviet forces, Sandrock succeeded in reaching US Army lines and was taken into American captivity. On 18 May 1945, he escaped from captivity and suc ceeded in reaching his family home near Bonn.

Herr Sandrock now lives in retirement near Cologne and is an official of the Ordensgemeinschaft der Ritterkreuzträger.

MAJOR ERNST HEINRICH THOMSEN

Ernst Thomsen entered military service in 1933 when he joined th *Reichsmarine.* He trained as a naval pilot and was commissioned with the ran of Oberleutnant zur See. During his pre-war naval career, Thomsen was one o the pilots on the pocket battleship *Admiral Graf Spee*. He served during th Spanish Civil War with the *Legion Condor* and was decorated with the Spanis Cross in Gold with Swords.

Thomsen's career with the navy was not to last, however, because th Commander-in-Chief of the *Luftwaffe*, Hermann Göring, decreed that anythin which flew must belong to the *Luftwaffe*, so the navy lost all of its trained pilots. Thomsen was transferred to the *Luftwaffe* in 1936.

During the Polish and French Campaigns, Thomsen served as a bomber pilot. Subsequently, he served with Kampfgeschwader 2 as Gruppenkommandeur in Italy and took part in anti-shipping strikes in the Mediterranean. In 1943–44, he served with III/KG 26 on the Western Front. The principal aircraft types flown by Thomsen during these anti-shipping operations were the Heinkel He 111, and the Junkers Ju 88 and Ju 188 bombers. For the success he achieved, he was decorated with the Knight's Cross on 24 October 1944. At the end of the war, Thomsen held the rank of Major.

In 1956 when the German armed forces were being reformed, Thomsen returned to active service with the *Bundesmarine* as a naval flyer. When he retired in 1972, he held the rank of Kapitän zur See, having served on the staff of the Kommando der Marineflieger and had become Lehrgruppenkommandeur in the Führungsakademie of the Bundeswehr.

OBERFELDWEBEL ALEXANDER UHLIG

Alexander Uhlig was born near Leipzig on 9 February 1919. He completed his schooling by gaining his Leaving Certificate (Abitur) in early 1937. After a period of service with the Reichsarbeitsdienst, the obligatory two-year period of military service prevented any continuance of his studies. In autumn 1937, Uhlig joined the first German Fallschirmjäger unit. This was to be the forerunner of Fallschirmjäger Regiment 1, which was formed in 1938. With this unit, Uhlig was to see action during the Sudetenland action and the occupation of Czechoslovakia.

Uhlig remained with Fallschirmjäger Regiment 1 during the Polish Campaign, followed by action in Norway. Following the airborne action on 14 April 1940 at Dombas in central Norway, he found himself in Norwegian captivity for around three weeks with all the other survivors from this action. On 14 May 1940, Uhlig and his platoon jumped during the first Battle of Narvik and thereafter he was decorated with the Iron Cross Second Class and the Narvik Shield.

After the successful conclusion of the Norwegian Campaign, Uhlig transferred to flying duties as a navigator and between 1941 and 1943 took part in over 170 operations, including the landings at Crete for which he was awarded the 'Kreta' campaign cuffband. During this period, Uhlig also qualified for the Flight Clasp in Gold and was awarded the Iron Cross First Class.

In June 1944, as the invasion of Normandy progressed, Alexander Uhlig was once again in action with a parachute unit. With the rank of Oberfeldwebel, he commanded 16 Kompanie/Fallschirmjäger Regiment 6. In Uhlig's sector of the front, Fallschirmjäger Regiment 6 was opposed by the US 90 Infantry Division. Heavy attacks on the regimental flanks saw Uhlig ordered to lead a small combat group of 30 of the tough German paras on a mission to attempt to stabilise the regiment's position. Uhlig's group took on, and defeated, an entire US battalion, taking over 230 prisoners, including the Battalion

Major Ernst Heinrich Thomsen was a successful anti-shipping pilot who later flew jets with the West German navy. (**Marineflieger**) *(Ernst-Heinrich Thomsen)*

Below left: Oberfeldwebel Alexander Uhlig served with Fallschirmjäger Regiment 6 during the Normandy campaign, winning the Knight's Cross. He was one of the few prisoners of war to escape from Allied custody, and reached his home without detection. (Alexander Uhlig)

Below right: SS-Obersturmbannführer Eggert Neumann served with the reconnaissance unit of 7 SS Freiwilligen Gebirgs Division **Prinz Eugen,** *winning the Knight's Cross for actions on the Eastern Front. (Arthur Charlton)*

Commander and eleven other officers. This was to be one of the last notable successes for the Germans in this sector of the front. In recognition of this tremendous achievement, Alexander Uhlig was decorated with the Knight's Cross of the Iron Cross on 29 October 1944.

Uhlig was captured shortly afterwards and, having spent some time in French and US prisoner of war camps, ultimately found himself at Camp 23 in Sudbury, Burton upon Trent, England. He was considered by the authorities to be a potential escapee and closely watched. On 22 April 1947, however, Uhlig did escape and made his way to Hull where he was able to stow away on a ship bound for Cuxhaven. His escape was initially covered up by the ruse of having a dummy take his place during roll call. By the time the escape was discovered three days later, Uhlig had already reached Germany. He then made his way through the less strictly controlled US zone and managed to cross the Russian lines undetected. By 28 April, he was home in Leipzig.

Allied records show that Uhlig was recaptured on 31 July 1947 but this is untrue; he was never retaken. So, despite claims to the contrary, at least one German prisoner of war did escape from a British Camp and succeeded in making his way home, albeit after the end of hostilities.

After his return, Uhlig took up his studies again, ten years late, at the Technical High School in Darmstadt. Despite unfavourable economic conditions, Uhlig completed his studies and gained his engineering degree. He worked for a number of well known German companies until his retirement just before his sixty-fifth birthday. Now living in Essen, he is an honorary member of the New Zealand Crete Veterans Association. Alexander Uhlig's military successes, his daring escape and his success in academic terms are a tribute to this plucky para's determination and strength of character.

SS-OBERSTURMBANNFÜHRER EGGERT NEUMANN

Eggert Neumann was born in Allenkirchen in December 1912, and served with 7 SS Freiwilligen Gebirgsdivision *Prinz Eugen* as commander of SS Gebirgs Aufklärungsabteilung 7. He was awarded the Iron Cross Second Class in 1940. This was followed by the award of the First Class on the Eastern Front in July 1941, shortly after the invasion of the Soviet Union.

By 1944, the division was heavily involved in combat against Tito's partisans in Jugoslavia, but in October 1944 it was sent to Belgrade to cover the flank of the German retreat through Jugoslavia. Having been involved almost entirely in security duties against partisans, the division was no match for the seasoned front line Soviet combat troops it met in action and suffered appalling casualties. Nevertheless, for his command of the Aufklärungsabteilung during these battles, Neumann was awarded the Knight's Cross on 3 November 1944.

Prinz Eugen was rebuilt after this mauling using drafts from other decimated units and was thrown back into the battle against Tito's partisans in January 1945. By the time it surrendered to the Red Army in May, its strength had been reduced to virtually nil.

Eggert Neumann died in retirement in Hamburg in 1970.

LEUTNANT WILLI HEINRICH

Born on 11 October 1914, Willi Heinrich was commissioned as a Leutnant in May 1943 after having seen service in Poland, France and Russia as a Panzer soldier. In September 1944, he was posted to Führer-Grenadier-Brigade *Grossdeutschland*, part of the *Grossdeutschland* Panzer Korps. Heinrich commanded 1 Kompanie of the Führer-Grenadier-Brigade Panzer Abteilung, equipped with the PzKpfw V Panther tank.

In East Prussia at the end of October 1944, a strong Soviet assault was pressing in the direction of Gumbinnen, south of Gross Watlersdorf. The Red Army was so strong by this time that tactical refinement was not required and sheer brute force was inevitably used. Heinrich's Panther Kompanie was thrown into a counter-attack against such a massed assault and he succeeded in penetrating the Soviet flanks and scattering them. A local encirclement of Soviet forces was achieved, but this success could only be short lived. By 27 October, the Führer-Grenadier-Brigade had been withdrawn and after a counter-attack in November which again successfully achieved its objective in capturing Goldap, albeit temporarily, the brigade went into reserve.

The Führer-Grenadier-Brigade was upgraded to full Panzer brigade status and next went into action during the Ardennes Offensive in December 1944, following which Heinrich was awarded the Knight's Cross on 9 December for his gallantry. He was also awarded the Wound Badge in Silver. The brigade was decimated during the Ardennes Offensive and at one point average comany strength was only 30 men.

In 1945, the brigade was expanded to divisional status and sent to Vienna to take part in the defence of the city. The Führer-Grenadiere-Division fought tenaciously but the unequal struggle was drawing to a close. The division was withdrawn from the line and retreated to Trakwein where it surrendered to US forces but was subsequently turned over to Soviet captivity.

HAUPTMANN GERHARD TSCHIERSCHWITZ

Born in April 1920, Gerhard Tschierschwitz enlisted into the *General Göring* Regiment in 1938 after leaving school and serving the statutory six months with the Reichsarbeitsdienst. Tschierschwitz served during the Western Campaign, in which Regiment *General Göring* operated in France and Belgium, the Flak unit especially distinguishing itself against Allied armour.

In 1941, the regiment was involved in Operation BARBAROSSA and acquitted itself well in the battles around Kiev and Bryansk. In 1942, it was reformed and expanded to divisional size, becoming the *Hermann Göring* Division. Elements were sent to Tunisia in November and the rest of the division to Italy in December. Tschierschwitz served with Panzer Regiment *Hermann Göring* in Sicily during the fighting withdrawal to Messina, from where it was eventually evacuated over to Italy. The Panzer Regiment served in Italy throughout 1943 and until 5 July 1944, when it was pulled out of the line and sent to the Eastern Front.

Leutnant Willi Heinrich served with Führer-Grenadier-Brigade **Grossdeutschland:** *the 'GD' emblems are visible on the shoulder straps. Heinrich is wearing the old-style field cap with its soft leather peak and flat wire woven insignia. (Willi Heinrich)*

Wearing the **Luftwaffe** *version of the special black Panzerjacke is Hauptmann Gerhard Tschierschwitz who won the Knight's Cross on the Eastern Front on 6 December 1944, whilst serving with the Hermann Göring Division. (Gerhard Tschierschwitz)*

The *Hermann Göring* Division had earned itself a high fighting reputation in Italy which it continued to enhance with its performance on the Eastern Front. Generalfeldmarschall Model himself congratulated the division on its achievements. In October 1944, the division was expanded to a full Panzer Korps. Late in October, whilst serving in East Prussia, it succeeded in throwing back the advancing Soviets at Nemersdorf on 21/22 of the month. By November, *Hermann Göring* was entrenched around Gumbinnen and for the next three months held back the Soviets, until their winter offensive opened in mid-January. On 10 December 1944, Gerhard Tschierschwitz was decorated with the Knight's Cross of the Iron Cross, for his command of 2 Kompanie of the Panzer Regiment during these hectic battles.

Eventually, the *Hermann Göring* units were cut off by the Soviet advance, at Heiligenbeil but were evacuated by sea to Denmark. The remnants were grouped with the remains of the *Grossdeutschland* Panzer Korps and fought in Saxony, where the Korps finally surrendered to the Red Army. Tschierschwitz was held in Soviet captivity from 1945 until 1953.

1945
FINAL DEFEAT

As the winter skies cleared and the Allied air forces attacked German troop and armour concentrations in the Ardennes, the death knell for Hitler's last great gamble was rung. By 16 January, American forces had linked up at Houffalize and the offensive was finally over. German losses are put at somewhere around one hundred and twenty thousand men and over 600 tanks. Losses in neither men or tanks could be made good at this late stage of the war and irreplaceable reserves of fuel had been expended.

By early February, the Canadians were advancing through the Reichswald. On 13 February, in one of the most controversial actions of the war, Dresden, a virtually undefended city, was devastated by over one thousand Allied bombers, dropping almost three quarters of a million incendiary bombs. Nearly a quarter of a million people, mostly civilians, died. A number of Allied prisoners of war were also killed. Later in February, Berlin received similar treatment when over three thousand tons of bombs rained down on the Reich's capital.

On 4 March, American tanks reached the Rhine north of Cologne and entered the town on the following day. Three days later, American troops captured the bridge at Remagen intact, though it subsequently collapsed. On 10 April, the Americans took Hannover. By the end of the month, German forces in Italy had surrendered to the Allies.

On the Eastern Front in 1945, fear of the type of retribution they expected from the Soviets led to much stiffer defence than in the West. In mid-January, the last great Soviet winter offensive had been launched by Zhukov and Koniev with over 160 divisions. German forces on the Eastern Front were now outnumbered by about five to one. On 17 January, Warsaw fell to Zhukov and by the latter part of the month, Germany had begun a massive evacuation exercise, when nearly two million troops and civilians were rescued by sea from East Prussia and Courland. Not all reached safety, however, and on 30 January, one of the worst-ever sea disasters occurred when a Soviet submarine sank the cruise liner *Wilhelm Gustloff* carrying over seven thousand refugees. Only a handful survived. The subsequent sinking of two other liners, the *Goya* and the *General von Steuben* brought the total loss of life to eighteen thousand.

By early February, the Red Army was laying siege to Breslau. Early the following month, 6 SS Panzerarmee launched a counter-attack in Hungary which achieved some initial success but this was very short lived and the Red Army's counter-attack was soon throwing the Germans back. On 12 March, Zhukov's troops captured Küstrin on the Oder and by the end of the month, the Red Army had taken Gdynia and Danzig and was also entering Austria.

On 6 April, Soviet units were entering the outskirts of Vienna and one week later, the city fell. On 9 April, Königsberg was taken by the Red Army. One

General Gerhard Matzky wears the postwar version of the Knight's Cross. He won the Cross as a Generalleutnant commanding 21 Infanterie Division in April 1944. (Gerhard Matzky.)

General der Fallschirmtruppe Eugen Meindl. A veteran of Narvik and Crete, Meindl won the Oakleaves in August 1944 and the Swords in May 1945 just before the war ended. (Heinz Springer)

week later, the might of the Red Army was thrown against Berlin and as the capital city of the Thousand Year Reich reeled under the Soviet onslaught, US and Soviet forces linked up as East met West at Torgau on the Elbe.

On 30 April, Adolf Hitler, his Greater German Reich shrunk to a few city blocks around the Chancellory building, took his life. The reins of power passed to Grossadmiral Karl Dönitz who brought the war to an end by authorising the signing of a surrender document at 02.41 hours on Monday, 7 May 1945.

During the closing months of the war, around 1147 Knight's Crosses, 194 Oakleaves and 41 Swords were awarded.

HAUPTMANN ROLF DÛE

Rolf Dûe, born in Hannover on 28 January 1915, began training in banking before commencing his six-months' service with the Reichsarbeitsdienst, which ended in March 1937. He entered military service in November 1937, joining Panzerjäger Abteilung 19. The following year, he was promoted to Gefreiter and nominated as a Reserve officer candidate. In June 1939, Dûe was promoted to Unteroffizier and two months later was a deputy Platoon Leader with the Signals Troop of Panzerjäger Abteilung 267, serving on the Siegfried line.

In February 1940, Dûe attended the Panzertruppe School at Wünstorf,

Clearly visible in this photograph of Hauptmann Rolf Dûe, commander of 1 Kompanie, Panzerjäger Abteilung 19, is the rare General Assault Badge for 25 engagements with the enemy. Interestingly, Dûe appears to be wearing non-standard metal insignia on his field cap. (Rolf Dûe)

Berlin. During his training, he was promoted to Feldwebel before commission-ed Leutnant in June of the same year. On commissioning he was posted to Panzerjäger Abteilung 19 in France, as Communications Officer.

As part of 19 Panzer Division, Dûe's unit was involved in Operation BARBAROSSA. Dûe received the Iron Cross Second Class on 21 July 1941. The division was to remain on the Eastern Front for the remainder of the war. Dûe was promoted to Oberleutnant in June 1942 and later that year, attended a course for Company Commanders at Schnelltruppen School in Versailles. On 3 January 1943, Oberleutnant Dûe was appointed commander of 3 Kompanie, Panzerjäger Abteilung 19, transferring to command 1 Kompanie on 16 March. During this period he was awarded the Wound Badge and in August, the General Assault Badge. In November of the same year, he was decorated with the Iron Cross First Class.

In May 1944, Dûe was promoted to Hauptmann and in October of that year, qualified for the General Assault Badge for 25 engagements with the enemy. By the end of 1944, 19 Panzer Division was involved in the defensive battles in Poland against the relentless Soviet advance. During the first two months of 1945, the division fought in the area around the Baranov bridgehead, near Breslau. In March 1945, Hauptmann Dûe was appointed Battalion Com-mander and was decorated with the Knight's Cross of the Iron Cross for his command of the unit during these ferocious battles. The award was made on 23 March.

With 1 Panzerarmee, 19 Panzer Division surrendered to the Soviets in May 1945. For the next three years Dûe was held in captivity in Czechoslovakia and Russia.

In April 1956, he returned to military sevice with the *Bundeswehr* and was sent to the US Armoured School at Fort Knox, Kentucky, where, in 1957, units of the newly resurrected German army were being trained. He was promoted to Major in 1958 and further promoted to the rank of Oberst in 1965.

OBERSTLEUTNANT MAXIMILLIAN FABICH

Max Fabich was born on 8 September 1914 as the son of a police official in Berlin. He attended the Friedrichs-Real-Gymnasium in Berlin from April 1924 until March 1933, and joined Infanterie Regiment 8 in Frankfurt on 3 April 1934, at the age of 20. He was commissioned as a Leutnant in April 1937 and this was followed by his transfer to 3 Kompanie of Infanterie Lehr Regiment in Berlin. In July 1939, Fabich was promoted to Oberleutnant.

On the outbreak of war, Fabich was a Platoon Commander in the newly formed Infanterie Regiment *Grossdeutschland*. Later, in June 1940, he took over command of its 3 Kompanie. He served in this capacity throughout the French and Jugoslavian Campaigns.

At the commencement of Operation BARBAROSSA, Oberleutnant Fabich and his Regiment formed part of Panzergruppe Kleist, reaching the central sector of the front in late June. In the months that followed, Fabich was several times wounded in action and in recognition of his gallantry and leadership, he was awarded the German Cross in Gold. The award was made in January 1942 and was followed by promotion to Hauptmann in February.

In one of the defensive battles around Orel during February 1942, Fabich was seriously wounded by a shell splinter and taken from the front to the hospital at Kuchwald, near Chemnitz. After several months convalescence, he returned to duty in September 1942 with Reserve Regiment *Grossdeutschland* in Kottbus. From April to December 1943 Fabich underwent General Staff training with 134 Infanterie Division in the central sector of the front. Following this, he was sent to the Kriegsakademie in Hirschberg and in April 1944, was promoted to Major.

In August 1944, Major Fabich was posted to Stammdivision *Grossdeutschland* in Memel, taking command of the rifle regiment. Later, he was appointed to command Panzer Fusilier Regiment *Grossdeutschland* and in March 1945, was promoted to the rank of Oberstleutnant.

On the night of 4/5 March 1945, the regiment was involved in a ferocious battle over farmland at Korschelken. Three times the farm land had changed hands during bitter hand to hand fighting. In the early hours of 5 March, Fabich personally led an attack which succeeded in throwing back the enemy for the fourth time. Fabich was repeatedly to be found at the thick of the fighting, urging his men on to even greater efforts. Soviet strength was growing ever stronger but Fabich, leading his men ever forward with machine pistol and grenades in hand succeeded in holding the enemy off.

During the course of 5 March, the enemy were considerably reinforced with heavy weapons, including tanks. Reconnaissance led Fabich to believe that a heavy assault in regimental strength was about to fall on his positions. Realising the danger, he immediately led his men in a spirited attack, once again leading from the front with total disregard for his own personal safety.

This is an early photograph of Oberstleutnant Max Fabich which has been retouched. Fabich was unaware that he had been awarded the Knight's Cross until after the war's end. The German Cross in Gold being worn appears to be the cloth embroidered type. (Max Fabich)

The Preliminary Certificate for Fabich's German Cross in Gold, bearing the signature of General Keitel. (Max Fabich)

When a machine-gunner next to him was wounded in the arm and unable to continue firing, Fabich snatched up the weapon and stormed forward against the enemy. Despite Fabich's great success in frustrating the enemy push, the overwhelming numerical superiority of the Soviet forces inevitably took its toll and the regiment was finally forced to withdraw.

In the course of this battle, Panzer Fusilier Regiment *Grossdeutschland* destroyed or captured 19 enemy guns and a number of heavy and light machine-guns. Only through the personal gallantry and the example set by Fabich to his men was this possible. This achievement was even more impressive as, due to manpower shortages, around 75 per cent of Fabich's forces was composed of stragglers.

Fabich was recommended for the Knight's Cross. The recommendation was approved on 19 April 1945. Such was the prevailing chaos at this late stage in the war, however, that Max Fabich did not find out about his award until well after the war's conclusion.

HAUPTMANN FRIEDRICH ANDING

Friedrich Anding was born in Göttingen on 26 June 1915. After schooling and service in the Arbeitsdienst, he was trained as an inspector with the State

Railway Service. On 3 November 1937, Anding commenced his military service with 14 (Panzerabwehr) Kompanie of Infanterie Regiment 82 in Göttingen.

In October 1938, he was posted to Infanterie Lehr Regiment in Berlin-Döberitz and was promoted to Gefreiter. In 1939, Anding, by then an Unteroffizier, was in command of a 3.7cm anti-tank gun as part of the elite newly formed Infanterie Regiment *Grossdeutschland*. He served throughout the French Campaign and in the Jugoslavian Campaign as an NCO with *Grossdeutschland*. By the commencement of Operation BARBAROSSA, Anding was with the regiment's 10 Kompanie, still in the anti-tank role.

Between January and April 1943, Anding attended the Panzertruppe training school at Wunsdorf after which he was commissioned as a Leutnant. Next, came training at Zossen as a Panzer company officer. Having completed this, Leutnant Anding was posted as a Training Officer with the *Grossdeutschland* Reserves at Cottbus before spending one year on the staff of the Officer Training School, also at Cottbus.

In December 1944, Leutnant Anding was back in action with Panzerjäger Abteilung *Grossdeutschland* as a troop commander. In March 1945, he was promoted to Oberleutnant and Abteilung Adjutant. Friedrich Anding was decorated with the Knight's Cross on 20 April 1945 for destroying six enemy tanks and five armoured cars in a single engagement with the use of the Panzerfaust hand held bazooka-type weapon.

Anding's decorations include the Iron Cross Second and First Classes, Infantry Assault Badge, German Cross in Gold, Infantry Close Combat Clasp in Silver, East Front Medal and, of course, the Knight's Cross. As well as these decorations, Anding was decorated with the Panzervernichtungsabzeichen, an award for the single-handed destruction of an enemy tank. A silver badge was awarded for the destruction of one tank, and a gold for five. Anding had three gold and three silver grade badges, a total of 18 enemy tanks destroyed. This closely rivalled the all-time record of 21.

Oberleutnant Anding returned to military service with the Bundeswehr in 1961 and finally retired with the rank of Hauptmann. He is still alive.

OBERLEUTNANT HEINZ HEUER

Heinz Heuer was born in Berlin in March 1918. After completing schooling he attended a course of further education, studying economics, before joining the Cadet Preparatory School in Potsdam.

On 1 November 1936, Heuer joined the Brandenburg Police School but had then to complete a two-year term of military service. His duties included service in Spain during the Civil War. On completion of his national service, he returned to police schooling in Potsdam, Eiche, Berlin and Police Technical School in Berlin. On completing his studies, he served with the Ordnungspolizei Headquarters in the Reich's Ministry of the Interior in Berlin and was attached to the Foreign Office. Heuer also served with the Abwehr and the Oberkommando der *Wehrmacht* Overseas Department. He became a courier to

Hauptmann Friedrich Anding closely rivals the record of 21 awards of the badge for single-handed destruction of an enemy tank, the three gold (upper) and three silver (lower) awards worn as braided strips on Anding's right sleeve, each with a small tank motif in the centre, indicating 18 awards. His **Grossdeutschland** *cuff title is also clearly seen on the same sleeve. (Friedrich Anding)*

Oberleutnant Heinz Heuer was one of the few highly decorated personnel of the German Military Police. In this photograph, he is an Oberfeldwebel of Feldgendarmerie and leader of a small Kampfgruppe leader in Berlin in 1945. (Heinz Heuer)

the Polizei Division and other police leadership staffs. Later, he served with all branches of the armed services and on temporary attachments to various embassies abroad.

Heuer's war service included duty with the famous *Brandenburg* Division and he saw service in Africa, Asia and Turkey. For his courier duties, Heuer became the first police recipient of the Motor Vehicle Drivers Badge of Merit in Gold.

During the battle of Berlin in 1945, Heuer served as an Oberfeldwebel of Feldgendarmerie (Military Police) in command of a small combat group. He was summoned to Hitler's Headquarters one day and tasked by Generaloberst Krebs with a special mission. He and his small band of men were to locate a suspected Soviet command post. Heuer had already carried out several dangerous missions and quickly set off on his new task with a small force of 28 men. On the night of 21 April, Heuer located the enemy post and after a short fire fight, captured it along with all the documents and maps it contained.

On his return trip, Heuer and his Kampfgruppe ran into trouble when they met a strong Soviet tank force. During the battle which ensued, 27 Soviet tanks were destroyed. Heuer's own personal score was an amazing 13 tanks.

Considering that his small unit had no anti-tank guns and had to destroy these Soviet tanks at point blank range using satchel charges, stick grenades and single shot Panzerfaust anti-tank rockets, their achievement was all the more impressive.

Generaloberst Krebs was delighted by Heuer's success and the information and maps which he had captured. For his achievement, Heuer was decorated with the Knight's Cross on 22 April and was given a battlefield promotion to Leutnant.

On 24 April, Leutnant Heuer was given a mission to take a personal written message from Hitler and deliver it by hand to General Steiner, for whose relief attempt Hitler anxiously waited. Heuer set off on a motorcycle but was shortly afterwards captured by a group of Soviet troops. Heuer managed to destroy the message by chewing it up and swallowing it. It was made clear to him and a number of other prisoners held by the Soviets that they were to be immediately executed. The prisoners were given spades and told to start digging their own graves. When they had completed this macabre task, a Soviet officer approached and offered them a last cigarette, telling them that this was the time to say their prayers. To the doomed men it must have seemed as if these prayers were being answered as an artillery barrage landed nearby and the Soviets ran for cover. Heuer lost no time in setting about the remaining guard with his spade and the prisoners ran off. All escaped although several were wounded during their flight.

Heuer's liberty was to be short-lived, however, and he was soon back in Soviet captivity as the last remnants of the Third Reich finally crumbled. He was held in Soviet camps in Berlin, then Siberia, and then in a punishment camp in Oms. Heuer ultimately ended up in the hands of the GPU in East Berlin but managed to escape to the Western Zone with the assistance of a sympathetic Russian officer.

After the war, Heuer became a consultant with the British Military Police in Berlin. In 1947, he moved to West Germany and again became an active police officer up until his retirement in 1967 through disability caused by his wounds.

APPENDIX ONE
THE DIAMONDS WINNERS

1.	Oberst Werner Mölders · Jagdgeschwader 51	15 July 194
2.	Oberst Adolf Galland · Jagdgeschwader 26	28 January 194
3.	Major Gordon Gollob · Jagdgeschwader 77	30 August 194
4.	Oberleutnant Hans Joachim Marseille · Jagdgeschwader 27	3 September 194
5.	Oberleutnant Hermann Graf · Jagdgeschwader 52	16 September 194
6.	Generalfeldmarschall Erwin Rommel · Heeresgruppe Afrika	11 March 194
7.	Korvettenkapitän Wolfgang Lüth · *U-181*	9 August 194
8.	Hauptmann Walter Nowotny · Jagdgeschwader 54	19 October 194
9.	Oberst Adalbert Schulz · Panzer Regiment 25	14 December 194
10.	Major Hans-Ulrich Rudel · Schlachtgeschwader 2	29 March 194
11.	Oberst Hyazinth Graf Strachwitz · Panzerkampfgruppe Kdr.	14 April 194
12.	SS-Gruppenführer Herbert Gille · 5 SS-Panzer Division *Wiking*	19 April 194
13.	General Hans Hube · 1 Panzer Armee	20 April 194
14.	Generalfeldmarschall Albert Kesselring · Oberbefehlshaber Süd	19 July 194
15.	Oberstleutnant Helmut Lent · Nachtjagdgeschwader 3	31 July 194
16.	SS-Obergruppenführer Josef Dietrich · 1 SS-Panzer Korps	6 August 194
17.	Generalfeldmarschall Walter Model · Heeresgruppe Mitte	17 August 194
18.	Oberleutnant Erich Hartmann · Jagdgeschwader 52	25 August 194
19.	General Hermann Balck · 4 Panzerarmee	31 August 194
20.	Generalleutnant Bernhard-Hermann Ramcke · Festungkommandant Brest	19 September 194
21.	Hauptmann Heinz-Wolfgang Schnaufer · Nachtjagdgeschwader 1	16 October 194
22.	Korvettenkapitän Albrecht Brandi · *U-967*	24 November 194
23.	Generaloberst Ferdinand Schörner · Heeresgruppe Nord	1 January 194
24.	General Hasso von Manteuffel · 5 Panzerarmee	18 February 194
25.	Generalmajor Theodor Tolsdorff · 340 Volksgrenadier Division	18 March 194
26.	Generalleutnant Dr Karl Mauss · 7 Panzer Division	15 April 194
27.	General Dietrich von Saucken · Armee Oberkommando Ostpreussen	8 May 194

APPENDIX TWO
THE SWORDS WINNERS

1.	Oberstleutnant Adolf Galland · Jagdgeschwader 26	21 June 1941
2.	Oberstleutnant Werner Mölders · Jagdgeschwader 51	22 June 1941
3.	Hauptmann Walter Oesau · Jagdgeschwader 3	16 July 1941
4.	Major Günther Lützow · Jagdgeschwader 3	11 October 1941
5.	Korvettenkapitän Otto Krestschmer · U-99	26 December 1941
6.	General Erwin Rommel · Panzergruppe Afrika	20 January 1942
7.	Hauptmann Heinrich Bär · Jagdgeschwader 51	16 February 1942
8.	Hauptmann Hans Philipp · Jagdgeschwader 54	12 March 1942
9.	Hauptmann Herbert Ihlefeld · Jagdgeschwader 77	24 April 1942
10.	Oberleutnant Max Ostermann · Jagdgeschwader 54	17 May 1942
11.	Leutnant Hermann Graf · Jagdgeschwader 52	19 May 1942
12.	Oberleutnant Hans-Joachim Marseille · Jagdgeschwader 27	18 June 1942
13.	Hauptmann Gordon Gollob · Jagdgeschwader 77	23 June 1942
14.	Oberfeldwebel Leopold Steinbatz · Jagdgeschwader 52	23 June 1942
15.	Generalfeldmarschall Albert Kesselring · C-in-C South	18 July 1942
16.	Hauptmann Werner Baumbach · Kampfgeschwader 30	17 August 1942
17.	Kapitänleutnant Erich Topp · U-552	17 August 1942
18.	Kapitänleutnant Reinhard Suhren · U-564	1 September 1942
19.	Hauptmann Joachim Müncheberg · Jagdgeschwader 51	9 September 1942
20.	Hauptmann Joachim Helbig · Kampf-Lehr-Geschwader 1	28 September 1942
21.	Generalmajor Karl Eibl · 385 Infanterie Division	19 December 1942
22.	Generalleutnant Hans Hube · XIV Panzerkorps	21 December 1942
23.	Major Wolf-Dieter Wilcke · Jagdgeschwader 3	23 December 1942
24.	Hauptmann Alfred Druschel · Schlachtgeschwader 1	19 February 1943
25.	Generalleutnant Hermann Balck · 11 Panzer Division	4 March 1943
26.	SS-Obergruppenführer Josef Dietrich · SS-Panzergrenadier Division *LSSAH*	14 March 1943
27.	Oberst Hyazinth Graf Strachwitz · Panzer Regiment	28 March 1943
28.	Generaloberst Walter Model · C-in-C 9 Armee	2 April 1943
29.	Kapitänleutnant Wolfgang Lüth · U-181	15 April 1943
30.	Oberst Walter Gorn · Panzergrenadier Regiment 10	8 June 1943
31.	Oberst Dietrich Pelz · Angriffsführer 'England'	23 July 1943
32.	Major Helmut Lent · Nachtjagdgeschwader 1	2 August 1943
33.	Oberst Adalbert Schulz · Panzer Regiment 25	6 August 1943
34.	Hauptmann Günther Rall · Jagdgeschwader 52	12 September 1943
35.	Generaloberst Hermann Hoth · C-in-C 4 Panzerarmee	15 September 1943
36.	General Josef Harpe · XXXI Panzer Korps	15 September 1943
37.	Hauptmann Walter Nowotny · Jagdgeschwader 54	22 September 1943
38.	Major Waldemar von Gazen · Panzergrenadier Regiment 66	3 October 1943
39.	SS-Obersturmbannführer August Dieckman · Panzergrenadier Regiment *Westland*	10 October 1943
40.	Generalfeldmarschall Günter von Kluge · C-in-C Heeresgruppe Mitte	29 October 1943
41.	Generalleutnant Gerhard Graf von Schwerin · 16 Panzergrenadier Division	4 November 1943

42.	Hauptmann Hans-Ulrich Rudel · Schlachtgeschwader 2 *Immelmann*	25 November 1943
43.	Oberst Hajo Herrmann · —	23 January 1944
44.	Major Heinrich, Prinz zu Sayn-Wittgenstein · Nachtjagdgeschwader 2	23 January 1944
45.	Major Erich Bärenfänger · Grenadier Regiment 123	23 January 1944
46.	Generalleutnant Dietrich von Saucken · 4 Panzer Division	31 January 1944
47.	SS-Gruppenführer Herbert Gille · SS Panzergrenadier Division *Wiking*	20 February 1944
48.	General Hermann Breith · III Panzer Korps	21 February 1944
49.	Oberstleutnant Franz Bäke · Panzer Regiment 11	21 February 1944
50.	Generalleutnant Hasso von Manteuffel · 7 Panzer Division	22 February 1944
51.	Oberstleutnant Egon Mayer · Jagdgeschwader 2 *Richthofen*	2 March 1944
52.	Hauptmann Gerhard Barkhorn · Jagdgeschwader 52	2 March 1944
53.	Oberst Franz Griesbach · Grenadier Regiment 399	6 March 1944
54.	Major Werner Streib · Nachtjagdgeschwader 1	11 March 1944
55.	Generalleutnant Richard Heidrich · 1 Fallschirmjäger Division	11 March 1944
56.	SS-Oberführer Hinrich Schuldt · 2 lett. SS-Freiwillige Brigade	25 March 1944
57.	Generalleutnant Georg-Wilhelm Postel · 320 Infanterie Division	26 March 1944
58.	Generalmajor Wend von Wietersheim · 11 Panzer Division	26 March 1944
59.	Generalfeldmarschall Erich von Manstein · C-in-C Heeresgruppe Süd	30 March 1944
60.	Generalfeldmarschall Ewald von Kleist · C-in-C Heeresgruppe A	30 March 1944
61.	Major Alwin Boerst · Schlachtgeschwader 2 *Immelmann*	6 April 1944
62.	Oberst Dr Ernst Kupfer · Schlachtgeschwader 2	11 April 1944
63.	General Hans Kreysing · XVII Armee Korps	13 April 1944
64.	General Hans Jordan · VI Armee Korps	20 April 1944
65.	SS-Brigadeführer Hermann Priess · 3 SS-Panzer Division *Totenkopf*	24 April 1944
66.	Kapitänleutnant Albrecht Brandi · *U-380*	9 May 1944
67.	Oberst Ludwig Heilmann · Fallschirmjäger Regiment 3	15 May 1944
68.	Generaloberst Georg-Hans Reinhardt · C-in-C 3 Panzerarmee	26 May 1944
69.	Oberst Horst Niemack · Panzer Fusilier Regiment *Grossdeutschland*	4 June 1944
70.	Oberstleutnant Alfons König · Grenadier Regiment 199 *List*	9 June 1944
71.	SS-Obersturmführer Michael Wittmann · 2/schwere SS-Panzer Abteilung 501	22 June 1944
72.	Generaloberst Eduard Dietl · 20 Gebirgsarmee	1 July 1944
73.	Oberstleutnant Josef Priller · Jagdgeschwader 26	2 July 1944
74.	Major Friedrich Lang · Schlachtgeschwader 1	2 July 1944
75.	Oberleutnant Erich Hartmann · Jagdgeschwader 52	2 July 1944
76.	Generalleutnant Smilo Freiherr von Lüttwitz · 26 Panzer Division	4 July 1944
77.	SS-Sturmbannführer Hans Dorr · SS-Panzergrenadier Regiment *Germania*	9 July 1944
78.	Major Anton Hackl · Jagdgeschwader 11	9 July 1944
79.	Generalmajor Rainer Stahel · Fester Platz Wilna	18 July 1944
80.	Oberstleutnant Theodor Tolsdorff · Grenadier Regiment 1067	18 July 1944
81.	Generalleutnant Fritz Bayerlein · Panzer-Lehr-Division	20 July 1944
82.	Oberstleutnant Johannes Steinhoff · Jagdgeschwader 77	28 July 1944
83.	SS-Gruppenführer Hermann Fegelein · 8. SS-Freiwilligen Kavallerie Division Florian Geyer	30 July 1944
84.	Hauptmann Heinz-Wolfgang Schnaufer · Nachtjagdgeschwader 1	30 July 1944

85.	SS-Gruppenführer Fritz von Scholz · 11 SS-Panzer Grenadier Division Nordland	8 August 1944
86.	SS-Obergruppenführer Felix Steiner · III germanische SS Panzer Korps	10 August 1944
87.	Generalleutnant Walter Fries · 29 Panzer Grenadier Division	11 August 1944
88.	Major Kurt Bühlingen · Jagdgeschwader 2	14 August 1944
89.	Generalleutnant Dr Johannes Mayer · 329 Infanterie Division	23 August 1944
90.	SS-Oberstgruppenführer Paul Hausser · C-in-C 7 Armee	26 August 1944
91.	SS-Standartenführer Kurt Meyer · 12 SS-Panzer Division *Hitlerjugend*	27 August 1944
92.	Generaloberst Robert Ritter von Greim · C-in-C Luftflotte 6	28 August 1944
93.	Generaloberst Ferdinand Schoerner · C-in-C Heeresgruppe Nord	28 August 1944
94.	SS-Brigadeführer Theodor Wisch · 1 SS-Panzer Division *LSSAH*	30 August 1944
95.	SS-Standartenführer Otto Baum · 2 SS-Panzer Division *Das Reich*	2 September 1944
96.	Oberst Hans Kroh · 2 Fallschirmjäger Division	12 September 1944
97.	General Wilhelm Wegener · L Armee Korps	17 September 1944
98.	Major Theodor Nordmann · Schlachtgeschwader 1	17 September 1944
99.	Generalleutnant Bernhard Ramcke · Festungkommandant Brest	19 September 1944
100.	General Otto von Knobelsdorff · XXXX Panzer Korps	21 September 1944
101.	Generalmajor Dr Karl Mauss · 7 Panzer Division	23 October 1944
102.	Major Werner Ziegler · Grenadier Regiment 186	23 October 1944
103.	Hauptmann Fritz Fessmann · Panzer Aufklärungsabteilung 5	23 October 1944
104.	General Hermann Recknagel · XXXXII Armee Korps	23 October 1944
105.	Generalleutnant Maximilian von Edelsheim · 24 Panzer Division	23 October 1944
106.	Generalleutnant Hans Källner · 19 Panzer Division	23 October 1944
107.	Oberst Werner Mummert · Panzer Grenadier Regiment 103	23 October 1944
108.	Hauptmann Josef Wurmheller · Jagdgeschwader 2	24 October 1944
109.	Generalmajor Dr Hermann Hohn · 72 Infanterie Division	31 October 1944
110.	General Hans von Obstfelder · LXXXVI Armee Korps	5 November 1944
111.	Generalleutnant Ernst-Günther Baade · 90 Panzer Grenadier Division	16 November 1944
112.	Oberst Karl-Lothar Schulz · 1 Fallschirmjäger Division	18 November 1944
113.	Oberleutnant Otto Kittel · Jagdgeschwader 54	25 November 1944
114.	Oberstleutnant Georg Frhr von Boeselager · 3 Kavallerie Brigade	28 November 1944
115.	General Helmuth Weidling · XXXI Panzer Korps	28 November 1944
116.	SS-Brigadeführer Hans Harmel · 10 SS-Panzer Division *Frundsberg*	15 December 1944
117.	General Traugott Herr · LXXVI Panzer Korps	18 December 1944
118.	Generalleutnant Alfred-Hermann Reinhardt · 98 Infanterie Division	24 December 1944
119.	SS-Obersturmbannführer Joachim Peiper · SS-Panzer Regiment 1	11 January 1945
120.	SS-Obergruppenführer Walter Kruger · VI Waffen-Armee Korps der SS	11 January 1945
121.	Oberst Wolfgang Kretzschmar · Jäger Regiment 24	12 January 1945
122.	Generaloberst Dr Lothar Rendulic · 20 Gebirgsarmee	18 January 1945
123.	Generalmajor Maximilian Wengler · 227 Infanterie Division	21 January 1945

145

124.	General Walther Nehring · XXIV Panzer Korps	22 January 1945
125.	Oberstleutnant Hermann Hogeback · Kampfgeschwader 6	26 January 1945
126.	Major Erich Rudorffer · Jagdgeschwader 54	26 January 1945
127.	General Friedrich Kirchner · LVII Panzer Korps	26 January 1945
128.	General Friedrich-Wilhelm Müller · LXVIII Armee Korps	27 January 1945
129.	SS-Oberführer Helmut Dörner · 4. SS-Polizei Division	1 February 1945
130.	Oberleutnant Ernst Wilhelm Reinert · Jagdgeschwader 27	1 February 1945
131.	Oberst Erich Walther · Fallschirmjäger Panzer Grenadier Division 'HG'	1 February 1945
132.	Generalmajor Max Sachsenheimer · 17 Infanterie Division	6 February 1945
133.	Generalfeldmarschall Gerd von Rundstedt · C-in-C West	18 February 1945
134.	Generalmajor Dietrich von Müller · 16 Panzer Division	20 February 1945
135.	General Friedrich Schulz · 17 Armee	26 February 1945
136.	Generaloberst Heinrich Gotthard · 1 Panzerarmee	3 March 1945
137.	Oberstleutnant Heinz-Georg Lemm · Füsilier Regiment 27	15 March 1945
138.	SS-Brigadeführer Otto Kumm · 7 SS Freiwillige Gebirgs Division *Prinz Eugen*	17 March 1945
139.	General Walter Hartmann · VIII Armee Korps	18 March 1945
140.	SS-Standartenführer Georg Bochmann · 18 SS-Freiwillige Panzer Grenadier Division *Horst Wessel*	26 March 1945
141.	Oberst Arthur Jüttner · Grenadier Regiment 164	5 April 1945
142.	Generalmajor Hermann von Oppeln-Bronikowski · 20 Panzer Division	17 April 1945
143.	Generalmajor Hellmuth Mäder · Führer-Grenadier-Division	18 April 1945
144.	Major Werner Schröer · Jagdgeschwader 3	19 April 1945
145.	Major Wilhelm Batz · Jagdgeschwader 52	21 April 1945
146.	Generaloberst Johannes Blaskowitz · C-in-C Netherlands	25 April 1945
147.	General Hermann Niehoff · Festung Breslau	26 April 1945
148.	Generalmajor Hermann-Heinrich Behrend · 490 Infanterie Division	26 April 1945
149.	General Karl Decker · XXXIX Panzer Korps	26 April 1945
150.	SS-Obersturmbannführer Otto Weidinger · SS-Panzer Grenadier Regiment *Der Führer*	6 May 1945
151.	SS-Obersturmbannführer Günther Wisliceny · SS-Panzer Grenadier Regiment *Deutschland*	6 May 1945
152.	SS-Oberführer Sylvester Stadler · 9 SS-Panzer Division *Hohenstaufen*	6 May 1945
153.	SS-Obergruppenführer Wilhelm Bittrich · II SS-Panzer Korps	6 May 1945
154.	General Fritz-Hubert Gräser · 4 Panzerarmee	8 May 1945
155.	General Eugen Meindl · II Fallschirm Korps	8 May 1945
156.	Oberstleutnant Karl Thieme · Panzer Grenadier Regiment 111	9 May 1945
157.	General Heinrich Frhr von Lüttwitz · XXXXVII Panzer Korps	9 May 1945
158.	General Otto Hitzfeld · LXVII Armee Korps	9 May 1945
159.	Oberstleutnant Josef Bremm · Grenadier Regiment 990	9 May 1945

The awards dated 9 May 1945 were all approved by the government of Grossadmiral Dönitz after the death of Hitler.

Only one award of the Swords was made to a foreign soldier, a posthumous honour to Japanese Admiral Isoroku Yamamoto, on 27 May 1943, shortly after Yamamoto's death.

APPENDIX THREE
CHRONOLOGY OF AWARDS

Figures shown for the award of the Oakleaves and above are as accurate as can be ascertained. However, in the case of the Knight's Cross itself, these figures are of necessity approximate. Awards may have been approved one month but not awarded until the following month.

Awards during 1939 were made in only two batches. The bulk of the awards during 1940 fall during the spring to late summer period, covering the invasion of Norway, then the campaign in the West. The number of awards also rose dramatically after the invasion of the Soviet Union in 1941 and after the invasion of Normandy in 1944.

THE KNIGHT'S CROSS

1939

September	10
October	11

1940

January	0
February	0
March	1
April	4
May	80
June	82
July	66
August	71
September	54
October	36
November	30
December	16

1941

January	10
February	6
March	17
April	12
May	31
June	65
July	111
August	111
September	120

October	110
November	89
December	104

1942

January	64
February	82
March	66
April	34
May	68
June	37
July	61
August	88
September	135
October	113
November	80
December	124

1943

January	133
February	76
March	115
April	159
May	75
June	57
July	77
August	165
September	137

October	119
November	131
December	154

1944

January	109
February	208
March	162
April	189
May	156
June	215
July	146
August	220
September	278
October	327
November	209
December	229

1945

January	166
February	255
March	283
April	312
May	131

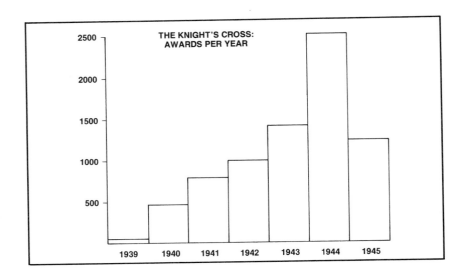

THE KNIGHT'S CROSS:
AWARDS PER YEAR

THE OAKLEAVES AND SWORDS AND OAKLEAVES

1940	Oakleaves	Swords		Oakleaves	Swords
July	1	—	March	5	1
August	0	—	April	6	1
September	2	—	May	4	2
October	2	—	June	8	3
November	1	—	July	4	1
December	1	—	August	7	2
			September	15	3
1941			October	12	0
January	1	—	November	8	0
February	1	—	December	19	3
March	1	—			
April	1	—	**1943**		
May	1	—	January	20	0
June	4	2	February	10	1
July	13	1	March	16	3
August	4	0	April	18	2
September	2	0	May	14	0
October	4	1	June	4	1
November	1	0	July	6	1
December	17	1	August	29	2
			September	16	4
1942			October	8	3
January	12	1	November	29	2
February	10	1	December	17	0

1944	Oakleaves	Swords		Oakleaves	Swords
January	21	4	November	32	6
February	27	4	December	15	3
March	28	10			
April	27	5	**1945**		
May	17	3	January	30	10
June	34	3	February	43	7
July	22	13	March	51	5
August	26	10	April	45	9
September	45	6	May	23	10
October	32	9			

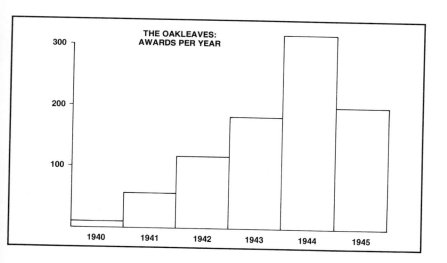

THE OAKLEAVES: AWARDS PER YEAR

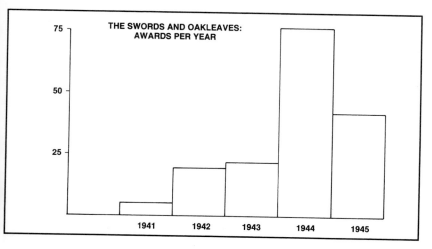

THE SWORDS AND OAKLEAVES: AWARDS PER YEAR

APPENDIX FOUR
AWARDS BY ARM OF SERVICE

As may be expected, the German army received by far the largest number of Knight's Crosses, at just over four and a half thousand. The *Luftwaffe* received just over one thousand seven hundred, the Waffen-SS just over four hundred and the *Kriegsmarine* just over three hundred. Although this may seem to be a very large proportion in favour of the Army, one must consider that the German army was a vast war machine compared with, say, the Waffen-SS or the *Kriegsmarine*.

If the figures are studied more carefully, we can see that awards were much more evenly distributed. The German armed forces had almost fifteen million men under arms during the war. A total of around seven thousand Knight's Crosses were awarded, thus giving a ratio of around 1-to-2150. The *Kriegsmarine* had approximately nine thousand men under arms and 318 awards, giving a ratio of approximately 1-to-2830. In the case of the Waffen-SS, with just under one million men under arms and 438 awards, the ratio is 1-to-2280. So, in fact, the ratio of awards to number of men under arms was very similar for all branches of the armed forces, with none receiving more than its 'fair share'.

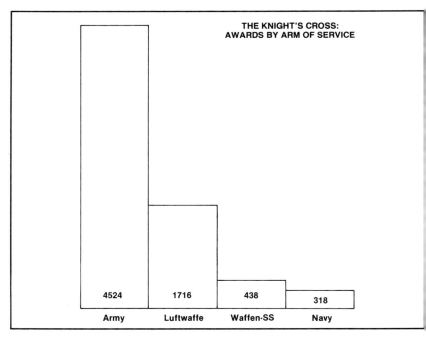

THE KNIGHT'S CROSS:
AWARDS BY ARM OF SERVICE

| 4524 | 1716 | 438 | 318 |
| Army | Luftwaffe | Waffen-SS | Navy |

On the subject of total numbers awarded, the Knight's Cross might seem more liberally awarded than the highest Allied awards such as the Victoria Cross (award ratio 1-to-49,500) or the Medal of Honour (1-to-28,500). One must remember that the Knight's Cross was the equivalent to not just the Victoria Cross, but also the Military Cross, Distinguished Flying Cross, etc. If we add together the total number of awards of all the major British gallantry awards, the combined ratio is 1 to 232. If we add all the awards of the Knight's Cross series, plus the German Cross in Gold, thus representing all the major German gallantry decorations, the award ratio is 1 to 600. On the other hand, if we take the highest German award as being the Diamonds, the award ratio is 1-to-94,000. This makes the Victoria Cross seem liberally awarded in comparison. This surely proves the point that direct comparisons between such awards as the Victoria Cross, a specific award for gallantry only, and the Knight's Cross, which could be awarded for a variety of meritorious deeds, are of dubious validity.

Considering the range of actions the Knight's Cross could be awarded to recognise, a total of just over seven thousand awards for armed forces of around fifteen million can in no way be considered liberal.

APPENDIX FIVE
AWARDS BY RANK

The following table shows the distribution of the Knight's Cross by rank, amongst the four branches of the Armed Services. Taken as percentages of the totals awarded to each of the services, this shows a remarkably even distribution amongst the various rank groupings. With the Oakleaves however, only 35 out of nearly nine hundred recipients were of non-commissioned rank. Only one of the 159 Swords recipients was non-commissioned. One must remember that many non-commissioned officers who were awarded the Knight's Cross were given battlefield commissions or were sent to Officer Training Schools shortly afterwards, so that several winners of the Oakleaves or Swords were still of very junior rank.

Rank	Army	Navy	Waffen-SS	*Luftwaffe*	Total
Generalmajor to					
Feldmarschall	400	23	17	62	502
Major to Oberst	1216	95	150	199	1660
Hauptmann	932	118	83	372	1505
Leutnant to					
Oberleutnant	1044	71	99	694	1908
Unteroffizier to					
Stabsfeldwebel	961	13	75	373	1422
Grenadier to					
Stabsgefreiter	223	1	14	16	254

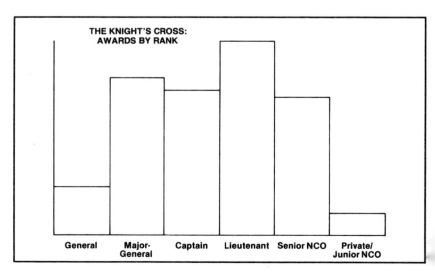

THE KNIGHT'S CROSS: AWARDS BY RANK

General | Major-General | Captain | Lieutenant | Senior NCO | Private/Junior NCO

TABLE OF COMPARATIVE RANKS

It should be noted that these are only approximate comparisons. In many cases there was no direct equivalent rank. For example, Reichsführer-SS was not a military rank comparable to field marshal. However, it was the highest possible rank in the SS, as was Generalfeldmarschall in the army or Grossadmiral in the navy.

BRITISH	GERMAN				US
Army	**Army/***Luftwaffe*	**Navy**		**Waffen-SS**	**Army**
Private	Grenadier/Flieger	Matrose		SS-Schutze	Private
—	Obergrenadier	—		SS-Oberschutze	Private First Class
Lance-Corporal	Gefreiter	Matrosengefreiter		SS-Sturmann	—
—	Obergefreiter	Matrosenobergefreiter		SS-Rottenführer	—
—	Stabsgefreiter	Matrosenhauptgefreiter	—		—
—		Matrosenstabsgefreiter	—		
Corporal	Unteroffizier	Maat		SS-Unterscharführer	Corporal
Sergeant	Unterfeldwebel	Obermaat		SS-Scharführer	Sergeant
Staff Sergeant	Feldwebel	Feldwebel		SS-Oberscharführer	Staff Sergeant
Warrant Officer Class 2	Oberfeldwebel	Stabsfeldwebel		SS-Hauptscharführer	Master Sergeant
—	Hauptfeldwebel	Oberfeldwebel		SS-Stabsscharführer	—
Warrant Officer Class 1	Stabsfeldwebel	Stabsoberfeldwebel		SS-Sturmscharführer	Warrant Officer
Second Lieutenant	Leutnant	Leutnant zur See		SS-Untersturmführer	2nd Lieutenant
First Lieutenant	Oberleutnant	Oberleutnant zur See		SS-Obersturmführer	Lieutenant
Captain	Hauptmann	Kapitänleutnant		SS-Hauptsturmführer	Captain
Major	Major	Korvettenkapitän		SS-Sturmbannführer	Major
Lieutenant-Colonel	Oberstleutnant	Fregattenkapitän		SS-Obersturmbannführer	Lieutenant Colonel
Colonel	Oberst	Kapitän zur See		SS-Standartenführer	Colonel
—	—	Kommodore		SS-Oberführer	—
—				SS-Brigadeführer	—
Brigadier-General	Generalmajor	Vizeadmiral		SS-Gruppenführer	Brigadier-General
Major-General	Generalleutnant	Konteradmiral		SS-Obergruppenführer	Major General
Lieutenant-General	General	Admiral		SS-Oberstgruppenführer	Lieutenant General
General	Generaloberst	Generaladmiral		—	General
Field Marshal	Generalfeldmarschall	Grossadmiral		Reichsführer-SS	General of Army

GLOSSARY OF TERMS

Where abbreviations are in common use, these are shown in brackets alongside the German term.

Abteilung (Abt.) battalion sized military unit.
Afrika Korps (D.A.K.) original title of Rommel's desert army, later known as Heeresgruppe Afrika.
Armee army
Armeegruppe army group
Armee-Oberkommando (A.O.K.) army high command
Artillerie (Art.) artillery
Aufklärung (Aufkl.) reconnaissance
Aufklarungsabteilung reconnaissance battalion

Bataillon (Bat.) battalion
Batterie battery
Befehlshaber commander
Begleit escort
Brigade brigade
Bundeswehr **(Bw.)** West German armed forces

Das Reich 2 SS Panzer Division, evolved from the SS-Verfügungsdivision.
Der Führer one of the original SS-VT Regiments.
Deutschland one of the original SS-VT Regiments.
Deutsches Kreuz German Cross, a military decoration.

Ersatz replacement, often used to describe divsional or regimental reserve pool.

Fahnenjunker officer cadet
Fähnrich senior officer cadet
Fallschirmjäger paratrooper
Flieger flyer, pilot
Flotille flotilla
Flotte fleet
Freiherr (Frhr.) baron
Freiwillige (Frw.) volunteer. Many of the SS divisions so prefixed did in fact contain many conscripts
Führer leader
Führer Begleit Hitler's escort
Führung leadership

Gebirgs mountain
Gebirgsjäger mountain troops
Geschutz gun
Geschwader squadron
Germania one of the original SS-VT Regiments
Grenadier (Gren.) motorised infantry private
Grossdeutschland (GD) premier unit of the German army
Gruppe group

Heer army
Heeresgruppe army group
Hitler Jugend (HJ) Nazi youth movement
Hitlerjugend 12 SS Panzer Division, composed mainly of ex-Hitler Jugend members

Infanterie (Inf.) infantry

Jäger (Jäg.) rifleman
Jagdflieger fighter pilot
Jagdgeschwader (JG) fighter squadron
Junkerschule Officer Training School

Kampf battle
Kampfgruppe battle group, a combat group of indeterminate size.
Kampfwagen (Kpfw.) tank
Kavallerie (Kav.) cavalry
Kaserne barracks
Kommandeur (Kdr.) commander
Kompanie (Komp.) company
Korps corps
Kradschützen motor cycle
Kraftfahr motorised
Kriegsmarine **(KM)** navy
Kriegsakademie staff college

Lehr training, instruction, demonstration
Leibstandarte (LSSAH) Hitler's elite SS bodyguard unit.
Luftwaffe air force
Luftflotte air fleet

Marine navy, naval

Mitte   centre

Nachrichten   signals
Nachtjagdgeschwader (NJG)   night fighter
 squadron
Nord   north

Oberbefehlshaber (O.B.)   Commander in
 Chief
Oberkommando (O.K.)   High Command
Ost   east

Panzer (Pz)   armour, tank
Panzerabwehr   anti-tank
Panzerjäger (Pz. Jäg.)   tank hunter
Panzer Korps   armoured corps
Panzergrenadier   armoured infantry
Polizei (Pol.)   police
Pioniere (Pi.)   engineers

Reichswehr **(Rw.)**   army of the Weimar
 Republic
Reiter   horsemen
Ritter   Knight
Ritterkreuz   Knight's Cross
Ritterkreuzträger   Knight's Cross Bearer

Schlachtflieger   ground attack pilot
Schnelletruppe   mobile troops
Schwere   heavy (the lower case 's' is
 grammatically correct for an adjective in

German, only the noun Schwer taking a
capital; the word is italicised in this book to
avoid confusion in an English text)
See   sea
Stab   Staff
Süd   south
Sturmgeschutz (Stug.)   assault gun
Standarte   regimental sized unit.
SS   Schutzstaffel
SS-Verfügungstruppe (SS-VT)   title by
 which Waffen-SS troops were formerly
 known.
SS-Verfügungsdivision   SS division which
 evolved into 2 SS Panzer Division

Totenkopf (TK)   Deaths Head, 3 SS Panzer
 Division

Unterseeboot   U-boat
Urkunde   citation, certificate

Verband   combination of units, group

Wache   guard
Wacheregiment   guard's regiment
Waffen-SS   SS combat units
Wehrmacht **(Wh.)**   armed forces
Zerstörer   destroyer, aircraft (Bf 110) or
 vessel
Zug   troop, platoon
Zugführer   Platoon commander

BIBLIOGRAPHY

Alman, Karl, *Ritterkreuzträger des Afrikakorps*. Erich Pabel Verlag, Rastatt, 1975.
Angolia, John R., *On the Field of Honour*, Vol. 1, R J Bender, San Jose, 1979.
—, *On the Field of Honour*, Vol. 2, R J Bender, San Jose, 1980.
—, *For Führer and Fatherland*, R J Bender, San Jose, 1976.
Argyle, Christopher, *Chronology of World War Two*, Marshall Cavendish, London, 1980.

Deighton, Len, *Blitzkrieg*, Jonathan Cape, London, 1979.
—, *Battle of Britain*, Jonathan Cape, London, 1980.

Fraschka, Günther, *Mit Schwertern und Brillanten*, Erich Pabel Verlag, Rastatt, 1970.

Hastings, Max, *Das Reich*, Michael Joseph, London, 1981.
—, *Overlord*, Michael Joseph, London, 1984.
Held, Werner, *Adolf Galland, Ein Fliegerleben*, Podzun-Pallas-Verlag, Friedberg, 1983.
H.I.A.G., *Wenn alle Brüder schweigen*, Munin Verlag, Osnabrück, 1973.

Kratschmer, Ernst G., *Die Ritterkreuzträger der Waffen-SS*, Verlag K W Schutz, Preussiche Oldendorf, 1955.
Klietmann, Dr Kurt G., *Deutsche Auszeichnungen*, Die Ordenssammlung, Berlin, 1971.
—, *Auszeichnungen des Deutschen Reiches*, Motorbuch Verlag, Stuttgart, 1984.

Lefevre, Eric, *Panzers in Normandy then and now*, Battle of Britain Prints, London, 1983.
Lehmann, Rudolf, *Die Leibstandarte im Bild*, Munin Verlag, Osnabrück, 1983.
Lenfeld and Thomas, *Die Eichenlaubträger 1940–1945*, Weilburg Verlag, Wiener-Neustadt, 1983.
Lucas, James, *Germany's Elite Panzer Force, Grossdeutschland*, MacDonald & Janes, London, 1978.
—, and Cooper, Matthew, *Hitler's Elite Leibstandarte SS*, MacDonald & Janes, London, 1975.

Mallmann-Showell, Jak P., *The German Navy in World War Two*, Arms & Armour Press, London, 1979.
Mitcham, Samuel W., *Hilter's Legions*, Leo Cooper, London, 1985.
Möller-Witten, Hans, *Mit dem Eichenlaub zum Ritterkreuz*, Erich Pabel Verlag, Rastatt, 1962.

Obermaier, Ernst, *Die Ritterkreuzträger der Luftwaffe*, Vol. 1, Dieter Hoffmann Verlag, Mainz, 1966.

—, *Die Ritterkreuzträger der Luftwaffe*, Vol. 2, Dieter Hoffmann Verlag, Mainz, 1975.

Proschek, Rolf, *Verweht sind die Spüren*, Munin Verlag, Osnabrück, 1979.

Range, Clemens, *Ritterkreuzträger der Kriegsmarine*, Motorbuch Verlag, Stuttgart, 1974.

von Seemen, Gerhard, *Die Ritterkreuzträger*, Podzun-Pallas-Verlag, Friedberg, 1984.

Schiebert, Horst, *Die Träger des Deutsche Kreuz in Gold*, Podzun-Pallas-Verlag, Friedberg.

—, *Die Träger des Deutsche Kreuz in Gold*, Vol. 2, Podzun-Pallas-Verlag, Friedberg.

Schneider, Jost, *Their Honour was Loyalty*, R J Bender, San Jose, 1977.

Spaeter, Helmuth, *Panzerkorps Grossdeutschland*, Podzun-Pallas-Verlag, Friedberg, 1984.

Snyder, Gerald S., *The Royal Oak Disaster*, William Kimber, London, 1976.

Weidinger, Otto, *Division Das Reich im Bild*, Munin Verlag, Osnabrück, 1981.

INDEX

158